A WINE TASTING COURSE

THE PRACTICAL WAY TO KNOW
AND ENJOY WINE

A WINE TASTING
COURSE

THE PRACTICAL WAY TO KNOW
AND ENJOY WINE

JOHN AND PATRICIA GOTTFRIED

DAVID McKAY COMPANY, INC.

New York

Library of Congress Cataloging in Publication Data

Gottfried, John.
A wine tasting course.

Includes index.
1. Wine tasting   I. Gottfried, Patricia, joint author.   II. Title.
TP548.5.A5G67   641.2′2   78–15010
ISBN 0–679–51451–1

9.27.79 Baker 9.42

1 2 3 4 5 6 7 8 9 10

DESIGNED BY JACQUES CHAZAUD

MANUFACTURED IN THE UNITED STATES OF AMERICA

ACKNOWLEDGMENTS

Although Pat and I have the satisfaction of seeing our names on the title page of this book, it could never have come into existence without the considerable help and encouragement of friends, contemporaries and professionals in the wine trade. We are especially indebted to Tom Ferrell, chief enologist at Inglenook Vineyards, for his help on the chemistry of wine; Chuck Mueller and Gerard Yvernault, of Kobrand Corporation; Margaret Stern, of Schieffelin Importers and Simi Vineyards; and Smitty Kogan of both the Champagne and Sherry Institutes. To them and everyone else we ever sipped and enjoyed wine with, we offer our thanks.

CONTENTS

Give me some wine and
    I will drink for today.
Teach me about wine and
    I will know forever.

I

FOUNDATIONS

The way to learn

about wine is not to read about it, but to drink it.

An obese and dissipated man once cornered me at a party and lectured me about wines. He enumerated the great bottles he had drunk: Romanée-Conti '49; Pichon Lalande '28 . . . like tombstones in a graveyard. He knew there were seven Grand Cru vineyards in Chablis, but in a tasting he could not have distinguished one of them from a Spanish "Chablis." His knowledge was pompous and useless; he didn't know what he was tasting. To a lesser degree, unfortunately, this is true of many people; they are more involved with the fame of the label than with the quality of the contents. A real knowledge of wine should involve the ability to recognize the quality and not be overly influenced by the prestige of the producer or vineyard. That is the very heart of this book. You have a choice in wine: You can study either the surface or the underlying form.

To look at the surface is to concern yourself solely with memorizing the relative merits of the different vintages, or the names of the châteaux and how they rank against one another according to the official government classifications.

If you choose to ignore the surface and instead concentrate on the underlying form, you become interested instead in how to recognize

1

a good wine: why it tastes good, and how it will improve. The wine stands on its own, totally without reference to the official hierarchy of wine.

Of course, this is simplistic. It is impractical to judge a bottle solely on its contents; else how could you ever read a wine list or buy from a wine store? The middle path, lingering a bit nearer the content than the form, is the heavenly mean.

The best way to do this is to build up a wine experience, a background from which to judge quality. The problem is where to begin. It is almost as if you must already know the subject before you can study it. A wine lover is not born with an innate knowledge like an Athena stepping full-grown from the forehead of her father Zeus. All of us have to learn bit by bit and try to build a coherent structure from the anarchy of choices we find.

To be perfectly honest, most other wine books are very bad things to try to learn about wine from. They haven't given enough thought to how the field should be organized. They often start alphabetically, beginning with the wines of the Azores and continuing on to Bordeaux —which does not seem to me to be a very effective method of teaching. Instead, the logical approach is to illustrate those characteristics that unify all wines, concentrating first on the similarities, not the diversity. Themes repeat themselves over and over again in wine.

Think how obvious it is. Add vinegar to a glass of wine and you will never again have any question what a spoiled bottle of wine tastes like. Add vodka and now you know what the bite of alcohol is like in a wine. That will also help show you what body means. Next think of overbrewed tea. The astringency, the bitterness, is tannin. Tannin is the same thing that preserves a red wine, and it is one of the ways to identify a young Bordeaux.

Once you know the tastes in a wine, the next thing to do is to try to learn about quality. Try three wines from Bordeaux: a regional (Mouton-Cadet); a commune (St. Julien); and a château-bottled wine (Ducru-Beaucaillou). You will learn more from that one tasting than from reading a dozen books.

Our errors will often teach us more than our successes. At first I could barely remember a good wine—they all tasted alike—but a bad one would stay with me for hours. It took years of trying first one wine and then another for me to gain enough experience to understand the errors I made, but after a while some forms and relationships made themselves apparent.

This is a light book. I've tried as much as possible to write as if I were talking to a friend. I am not out to impress you. The plainer I speak, the more you'll understand. Elements in wine are not mysterious, they are rational and understandable—once you see the underlying structure. You do not have to memorize a thicket full of names or other such schoolboy tasks. That is not what real wine knowledge is about. Instead, you slowly build up a tasting experience and get a clear idea of what a good wine is, how it will develop, what is meant by body, breed, finesse, tannin and other terms that many people find hard to pin down. The point is that these terms are objective and can be demonstrated to you by simple relationships that you can observe for yourself.

The tastings are the key, the unique contribution of this book. Every time I talk in depth about some wine area like Bordeaux or discuss the effect that aging has on a wine, that section will be immediately followed by a tasting to explain what I am talking about. The tasting is an involvement, like an actor walking off the stage and into the audience to break down the barriers that separate the reader from the play.

The tastings are structured so that a choice is offered. There are *preferred* wines and *alternatives*. The preferred wines are ones that are reasonably priced and widely available; you are as likely to find them in Chillicothe, Ohio, as in Chicago. In most of the tastings, as an alternative, there is also a *premium* wine suggested. They are more expensive and possibly harder to find. They don't illustrate the point any better than the reasonably priced "preferred" wines, but because more care and expense went into making them, you will probably find them more complex and interesting.

Wine is nothing like cars but is very much like art. In cars, you pretty much get what you pay for. In art, you can overpay or you can get great bargains; so each tasting is followed by a "caveat imbiber," some observations on consumerism which tell you where to find the more exciting wines and when to go against the trends.

The tastings are progressions. Each builds on the learning of the previous one, until what you have learned resembles a pyramid with each block representing a finer and more informed judgment as you progress upward from the base.

We start of course at the most basic level, which is: What are you tasting when you taste a wine? That includes the tannin and the alcohol level and all those related things. Once you can recognize those scien-

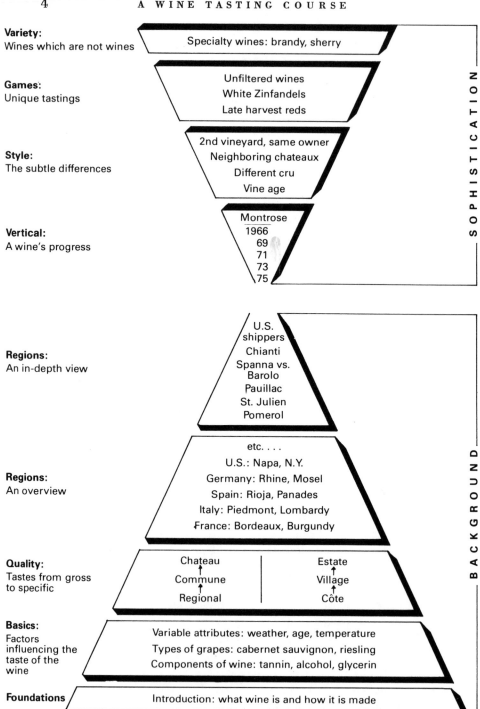

Variety:
Wines which are not wines

Specialty wines: brandy, sherry

Games:
Unique tastings

Unfiltered wines
White Zinfandels
Late harvest reds

Style:
The subtle differences

2nd vineyard, same owner
Neighboring chateaux
Different cru
Vine age

Vertical:
A wine's progress

Montrose
1966
69
71
73
75

SOPHISTICATION

Regions:
An in-depth view

U.S.
shippers
Chianti
Spanna vs.
Barolo
Pauillac
St. Julien
Pomerol

Regions:
An overview

etc. . . .
U.S.: Napa, N.Y.
Germany: Rhine, Mosel
Spain: Rioja, Panades
Italy: Piedmont, Lombardy
France: Bordeaux, Burgundy

Quality:
Tastes from gross
to specific

Chateau
↑
Commune
↑
Regional

Estate
↑
Village
↑
Côte

Basics:
Factors
influencing the
taste of the
wine

Variable attributes: weather, age, temperature
Types of grapes: cabernet sauvignon, riesling
Components of wine: tannin, alcohol, glycerin

Foundations

Introduction: what wine is and how it is made

BACKGROUND

tific components, the best thing is to familiarize yourself with the tastes of the main grapes because they comprise the basic taste of the wine. That is step two in the diagram and chapter 4 in the book. Next I show how wine changes with weather, age, temperature summation, etc., and with that you can say you are over the basics.

The next stage is learning to recognize quality. That is what I meant when I talked about testing a regional, a commune and an estate- (château) bottled wine side by side. What you will notice is that the smaller an area a wine is from (ideally from one specific vineyard), the better it will be.

From here we move on to what can be broadly described as regional studies. We survey the major wine regions such as Italy, France and California, and try to show what common themes give each area individuality. Each region is like a totally different school of painting; even given the same tools, the results are often drastically different. A Riesling from Germany or an estate-bottled wine from Burgundy will not taste at all like the same grape grown in the Napa Valley (California), and the contrast is one of the most enduringly interesting aspects of enjoying wine.

Several of the important regions we will visit twice, the second time in much greater depth and with a repeat emphasis on the important leitmotifs of the areas. It is interesting how simple a thorough knowledge of wine really is. It's not like studying nuclear physics or medicine. Even with the second visits, when some pretty sophisticated points are cropping up, they have the obviousness of natural logic.

GETTING OUR FEET WET

Wine would be relegated to the status of such novelties as ginger-root tonic or seaweed soup if it wasn't alcoholic. Alcohol is both the medium on which the taste and bouquet float and also a release in itself. Man has leaned heavily on it for support in times of distress at least as often as religion, and it has proven as much of a comfort when not used promiscuously. Man, in recognition of this, has made Bacchus a God and carried his God with him wherever he went. I know of an Egyptian Clos des Pyramides and I recall an Afghan wine that kept me warm at night and foggy in the morning.

The number of different grapes that are cultivated is astonishing, and this variety is probably the chief cause of all the confusion about wine. It is easy to survey but difficult to understand such a vast array. It is best to start with just two factors that determine a wine's qualities. One is the grape used, and the other is the care employed. Most wine is meant merely to lubricate a meal. Cost is the dominant criterion, and so for such wines grape varieties are chosen that will yield the largest acceptable quantity of juice. The wine produced is meant to be drunk young and as thoughtlessly as possible. This is the wine that is put down automatically on your table in the taverna in Italy. It also includes the typical American jug wine, although a few of these are made well enough to fit into a higher class.

Jug wines or vin ordinaire would hardly cause one to dedicate himself to a lifetime of serious imbibing. Such is the province of the more expensive wines. The best wines are usually made from a single variety of grape or a blend with one type dominating. In general, unblended wines seem to have greater ambitions.

By a management technique called perceptual mapping, there is another way to get an overview of wines. Like Gaul, all wines can be divided into four parts. You can say that wines are light and fruity; light and dry; heavy and fruity; and heavy and dry.

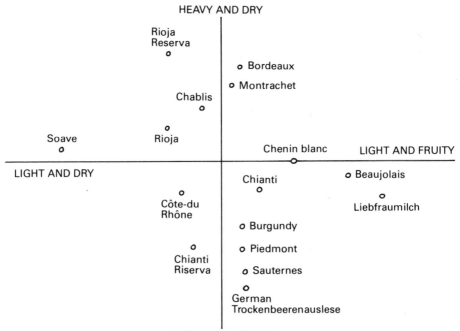

In other words we are dividing wine into two components: *weight* and *relative sweetness*. Weight, in wine terminology, is synonymous with body—it is a matter of intensity, not poundage. Milk has body; water does not. Beaujolais has very little weight, that is, not much intensity. It is light and easy to drink and is consumed almost without thought—except for the pleasure it gives you. An equally light wine, but dry rather than fruity, would be a white Italian Soave. You will find that fruity wines are wonderful for quaffing but dry wines complement food better.

Heavy-bodied wines are usually wines with ambition. They are intense and complex, not delicate. The best red and white wines have this quality of bigness. The Cabernet Sauvignons (that's the grape type) from California or Bordeaux are dry, aristocratic wines. They have fruit but they also have a power to them like a rigid backbone. Burgundies, by contrast, rely more on fruit and a certain supple roundness with which you will become familiar in succeeding chapters. They have a softer texture that is quite recognizable when you drink them.

To a great extent, what a wine becomes is in the hands of the winemaker. By using different techniques, he can make the wine heavier or lighter, sweeter or drier. He has control over its basic characteristics, but just because he makes a sweet wine doesn't mean it is a *good* sweet wine. That quality is in the berry.

All that is necessary to make wine is for the grape to ripen and its skin somehow to be pierced, thus allowing wild yeasts to get at the fruit sugar. Like the hungry little beasts they are, the yeasts gorge themselves on the sugar and transform it into alcohol plus CO_2. This deceptively simple metamorphosis is called fermentation. It is not limited

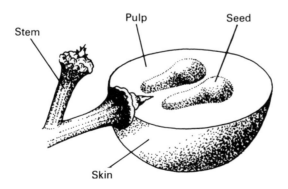

Stem · Pulp · Seed · Skin

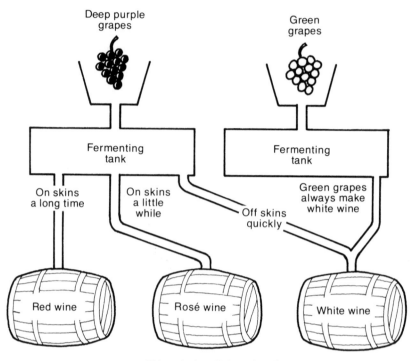

Either dark *or* light colored grapes
can make white wine.

to grapes. Any sugar-rich fruit will ferment—even sumac berries can make an interesting brew—but strictly speaking, we limit the use of the term "wine" to fermented grape juice.

All grapes are built the same way. They are composed of a seed enclosed in pulp and surrounded by a skin. The grapes come in basically two colors: black and green. The black may vary from deep purple to rust and the green from rust to yellow. *The majority of grapes have white juice; it is the skins that give them the color.*

A red wine can only come from a red or purple grape. Once the berry is crushed and the juice has begun to ferment, it is left to rest with the skins. The alcohol dissolves the pigmentation from those skins and makes the wine dark red. If the skins are removed before the juice has had a chance to pick up color, then a black grape will give you white wine.

A rosé is a compromise. It is not a blend of red and white wines*,

---

* Or shouldn't be.

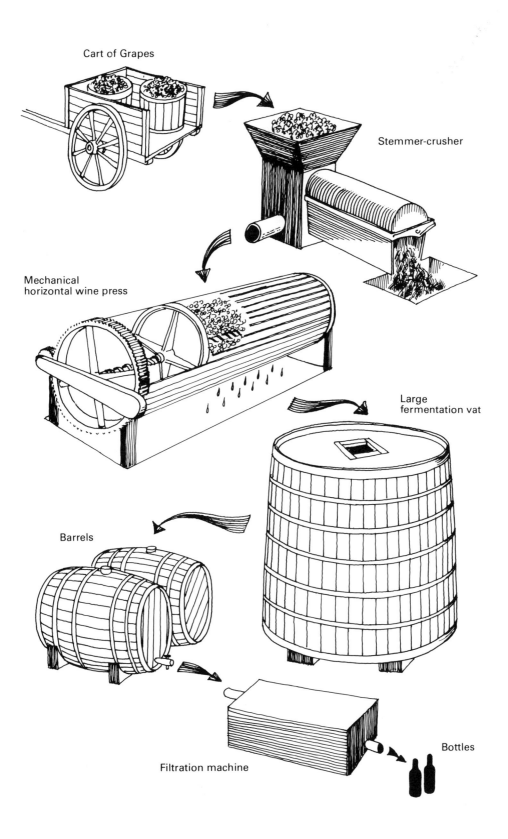

Cart of Grapes

Stemmer-crusher

Mechanical
horizontal wine press

Large
fermentation vat

Barrels

Filtration machine

Bottles

but a red wine that is left on the dark skins only long enough to pick up a hint of color. Then the juice is removed so it can complete its fermentation alone. Much of the heavy, complex tastes of great wines are carried in the skins, so a rosé must pay the price of being lighter and less sophisticated.

White wines made from green grapes can remain on their skins for some time. Few of them do however. The skins would give them too much character, and that is only desirable in a great wine. Most whites are made for their freshness and youth, and they come off the skins posthaste after crushing.

After this first, violent fermentation, the wine is allowed to sit undisturbed, usually until the following spring. During that period the murky wine partially clarifies. The floating debris sinks to the bottom. The wine is then racked off the lees (skins, pits and other deposits) and put into barrels to age. Less expensive wines go into metal or glass tanks or large wooden barrels. The type of wood is important. Small oak casks are preferred—new ones—especially if they are from Limousin or Nevers in France. The cost is quite high—about $170 each for a 55-gallon barrel—but the oak does impart a definite, positive taste to the wine. Ideally, barrels should be used only once. One of the most famous growths in all Bordeaux, Château Ausone, uses its barrels over and over again, but its reputation is declining and many people believe it is due to this reuse of barrels.

Premium red wines may stay in wood two or three years. In some countries (Spain, Argentina) it may be longer, but since wood breathes, too much oxygen may be absorbed and the wine can go flat—oxidize. White wine, which owes much of its appeal to freshness, seldom stays in wood longer than six to twelve months. The fullest and most complex of all white wines, a Chardonnay, can stay 12–18 months. The wine is then drawn off, filtered for clarity, and bottled. Less expensive whites may never touch wood at all.

Filtering removes the dead yeast and other particles from the wine, making it clear. Too fine a filter can rob the wine of taste; too coarse a filter will leave the wine cloudy. Over time, a good wine will throw off more sediment, which will collect like a sandy deposit in the bottom of the bottle. Don't be upset—it is usually a sign of quality. The method for getting rid of it is described under "decanting" in the Exterior Knowledge chapter.

Once the wine is in the bottle, the winery may release it immediately or may hold it for a period of aging in its own cellars. Storage ties up capital, so the tendency is to sell the wine as soon as possible. The amount of additional aging required is a function of the variety of grapes used, the weather that year, and the style the winemaker is trying for. The proper amount of aging presents one of winemaking's most intriguing problems, one we will be returning to frequently in the book.

Consumerism. Usually "consumerism" follows a tasting in this book, but in this first chapter there is no tasting. Still, there are some points to be made here.

It is appropriate to start by quoting the Bible, Matthew (7:15):

> Beware of false prophets, which come to
> you in sheep's clothing, but inwardly they
> are ravening wolves.

Let that stand for the wineshop that still has the 99¢ bottle. There are bargains in wine, but anything that cheap has to be pure swill. No one gives anything away for free. There are basic fixed costs. Even ignoring the wine, the wine industry must still cork, bottle, label, pack, transport, insure, pay taxes and cover middleman profits before the wine gets to you. Most of these costs do not vary with the quality of the wine; they are fixed. There is a price floor under which acceptable wines can no longer be delivered, and that floor can only be lowered by utilizing economies of scale (as in domestic jug wines) or by someone's taking a loss. That price floor is about $1.75 a bottle. Below that you must expect a chancy wine.

To get the best value, find the best wine merchant in town. He has more experience than a liquor-store operator whose only knowledge of wine comes from the salesmen who call on him. The wine merchant is an enthusiast, and because wine is an infectious cult, his clerks are usually involved too. He loves making converts. Not only is it good business, but—in case you haven't noticed—wine is like a religion, and one cannot help but try to get others to take up the true faith.

You should break up your wine buying into two categories: wine for everyday drinking, and wine for special occasions. You will be buying your daily wines in sizable quantities, so they should be inexpensive. A few dollars—no more. At prices higher than this you may feel uncomfortable about pulling out those extra bottles when you want them. *One of the most important lessons of this book is that you don't have to overspend to get quality.* In fact, price may be an indication, but it is never a guarantee. One of my best friends, an Austrian whose tastes

I totally respect, has never in his life spent more than three dollars for a bottle of wine. Good taste is not a matter of price, it is a matter of knowledge. It is ignorance that gives cupidity its chance.

The second type of wine you will be buying are the premium wines for special occasions. These are the wines that send wine writers into fits of fluffy prose. Don't mix the two of them up. Someone spent a good deal of time, skill and patience trying to make a fine wine from that ragged little fruit, so it would be a crime to consume it thoughtlessly. Not that I think that is possible. A great wine is so noticeably good that even the most inexperienced imbiber is aware that it is special. The only people who aren't able to appreciate and understand a fine wine are people whose span of attention didn't last as long as the bottle did. In other words, they weren't interested. So put out of your mind any worries you might have about the delicacy of your palate. Wine enthusiasts are not people with mystical taste buds. They are just enthusiasts like any other hobbyists.

II

EXTERIOR
BUT INDISPENSABLE
KNOWLEDGE

This chapter contains the unavoidable advice that I myself never enjoy reading. It deals with the form and the how-to's rather than with the wine itself. I know that I'd prefer uncorking the bottle and simply drinking down the wine, but there is a lot of value in knowing that a bottle's shape tells you where a wine is from, that a cork is more a guarantee than a label, and even that the glass you choose influences the taste of the wine.

Let me start off by sounding like a pompous old professor: You ought to take notes on the wines you drink. It is work and it detracts from the immediate pleasures, but you will find that unless you record your reactions to a wine in an orderly fashion, you will retain only vague impressions of it. You can remember your first hundred bottles in general terms but after that . . . confusion. So if you are serious you will take notes, and if you are not you will go on until such time as you will find notes to be useful. It's a case of water (wine) finding its own level.

If you plan to keep notes there are special cellar books on the market for from ten to sixty dollars. They serve as an elegant but functional record of what wines you have had or want to have in your cellar, and provide pertinent information about each one. Special cellar books are as unnecessary as they are overpriced. I should know: I wrote one of them. For myself I use a simple three-by-five-inch card set up in the following manner:

(1) Ayler Kupp   White
  (2) Feinste Auslese, Germany   (3) 1969
  (4) Steiger

(5) 4/75:....wine shop   (6) 1 case

(8) 10/77:   (7) $26/case (good buy)

                (9) 12 10

(10)

                      (11) 17/20

---

(1) name of wine.
(2) classification/origin (for example, Bordeaux, California Cabernet Sauvignon, etc.)
(3) vintage.
(4) name of bottler or shipper.
(5) where and when purchased.
(6) quantity purchased.
(7) case/bottle price.
(8) date tasted.
(9) number of bottles remaining.
(10) your personal description of the wine.
(11) a relative rating of the wine.

You will notice that I keep much more information than just the vineyard and the year. The when's and where's of purchase and the price are more than historic information. The price and your reactions tell you whether you will want to re-purchase the wine, and since the wines you will be most involved with are available year after year, you should know your past reactions to them. Such notes will be invaluable in deciding which is a superior value, 1971 Phélan-Ségur at $4.00 or Calon-Ségur 1970 at $6.00.

The most important record to keep is of the general characteristics of the wine you study. It develops and disciplines your own perceptions, because in re-reading your comments you will feel the inadequacy of earlier subjective descriptions, like "pleasant" or "good," and will replace them with more objective terms like "fruity" or "balanced." Also, there is nothing as reassuring as coming across some early judgment at a later date and finding out how perceptive you were. If you try a wine and note the strong presence of tannin, and say "too young, try again in one year," and then in a year it has mellowed, well, you've both matured.

When you taste a wine, discuss it, talk about how it feels, what it makes you think of, and so on. Try to describe it first in your own terms, even if they are just "good" or "bad". Then try less subjective terms:

Are there many tastes? (complex);
Do they fit together? (balance);
Are they subtle? (finesse);
Is it harsh? (tannic);

and so on. But most of all, overcome your modesty and don't be intimidated by your inexperience. You are stating your own reactions and learning to recognize landmarks in an unfamiliar land. Don't worry about making a mistake. Most wines you will be trying will be sound, good wines. A bad bottle is rare and announces itself so loudly you can scarcely miss it. After trying a few good wines you will have the basic tastes down pat. From then on it is a matter of expanding your experience and refining your taste. So talk about the wine, exchange impressions with friends, write them down. Be conversational, especially at first, because you will teach as you learn.

Now let's change gears. Before you involve yourself in the wine, involve yourself with the bottle. In most cases the shape or color of the bottle will tell you its origin. One speaks of a Burgundy-shaped bottle, which is slightly pudgy, stoop-shouldered and a slightly sickly green (for red wine, that is), while a Claret (the English name for Bordeaux) is leaner, with high shoulders and with a deeper, healthier green cast.

The case is made even better in Germany. The shape of both Rhine and Moselle bottles is identical, distinctively tall and thin, but you could never mistake one for the other. Moselle is sparkling green and Rheingau a stern brown. Italy and other countries have also, for the most part, evolved their own sizes and shapes. Interestingly, American wines that ape the style of a Burgundy or a Bordeaux usually also copy the shape of the bottle.

The label is the birth certificate and pedigree of the wine. It is also a marketing gimmick, so while what it states must by law be true, it will also be presented in its most appealing interpretation. Each country, indeed each region, has its own laws regarding labeling—which will be gone into in confusing detail later on—but for now just check how specific the label is. Is a vintage date shown, or is the wine a blend

BOTTLE SHAPES

Sherry

Bordeaux

Burgundy

Chianti Fiascho

Champagne

Rhine and
Moselle

of several years? Is the wine sold as a regional wine, or does the label tell you the specific vineyard? Does it name the grapes from which it was made, or only the region of origin? You can expect to find that the more specific and detailed the label, the better the wine will be.

HANDLING THE WINE

The handling of wine has always been surrounded by ritual—ritual which is often considered silly or pompous because it is not understood. The purpose of special wine procedures is to allow the wine to develop and be shown to its fullest advantage. The more sophisticated and venerable the wine, the more care should be taken in its presentation. On the other hand, gestures unnecessary for the enhancement or presentation of a wine have no purpose and should be avoided. Treat a great wine with respect—it is worthy of study—but drink a simple young wine without fanfare.

Each step in the ritual of wine-handling accomplishes a specific goal. For example, standing an older bottle upright a day or two before serving it allows the sediment to settle to the bottom of the bottle so that it will not impart a bitter taste to the wine.

You may want to decant the wine. Aside from merely being an elegant way of serving wine, decanting serves two purposes: It aerates the wine, and separates the wine from any sediment. The act of pouring the wine into a decanter exposes more of the surface to air than does simply uncorking it. The benefit of this has recently been hotly debated. The old gospel was that this was beneficial for young wines. The additional exposure to oxygen accelerated in a crude way the development of bouquet and aroma, and made the wine less harsh and more pleasant. The revisionists now argue that this is all false, that exposure to air only causes the wine to lose quality. If the wine is bad (has a slight hydrogen sulfide nose) it may appear better. If it is good, it is just losing quality. Maynard Amerine, one of the most knowledgeable professors at the University of California at Davis, agrees, and points out that no esterfication* or significant beneficial chemical change can take place in less than two to five years. Still, the point is far from proven, and many of us still prefer the bottle uncorked and the wine poured beforehand. It is a case where you must

---

* The interaction of acids and alcohol in wine produces esters which are commonly believed to be a chief source of a wine's aroma.

judge for yourself. Both camps agree, however, that oxygen will hasten the demise of a mature wine. If you have a 1949 Corton, say, you may be flirting with danger if you decant it far in advance. Care must be taken that these older wines do not breathe too long, even in the bottle.

The main and incontestable advantage of decanting is that you can separate the wine from the sediment at the bottom of the bottle. The classic method of decanting makes use of a candle or small, intense light behind the bottle's neck, permitting you to see sediment approaching the mouth of the bottle so you can stop pouring.

Even before you decant the wine, check the cork. It can tell you a great deal about the wine. Quality wines generally have a long cork as added insurance against air passage. Corks are subject to deterioration, drying out, cork worm and a series of other afflictions which could indicate that the wine has spoiled. However, most of these are rare. Check to see if the cork has printing on it. Fine wines frequently have the vineyard name and vintage on the cork as an added sign of authenticity. Test the firmness of the cork and note the depth of color it has taken from the wine. Smell the cork end. You should be able to detect some of the wine's character, which the cork ought to have absorbed over the years.

Certain facts are so obvious that we tend to overlook them. The common practice among serious wine drinkers (but unfortunately not among waiters) is to fill the glass no more than one-third full. This permits the bouquet to gather and be retained in the rest of the glass, which could not happen if the glass was totally full. It is precisely for the retention of the aromas that good glasses are curved back in at the top, the overall shape being rather like a tulip.

One of the absurdities perpetuated by fashion has been the belief that a different type of glass is necessary for each wine. If you have enough room to store several hundred glasses, it is a pleasant enough indulgence, but it is totally uncalled for. "One size fits all" works quite well in wine. A large glass of ten to fourteen ounces will hold two to three ounces of wine. As would be expected, it should have a base and stem and be recurved inward at the top. Wine drunk from fine (thin) crystal seems to taste more subtle than when served from a thick glass. Maybe the setting enhances the gem; other than that I can't offer an explanation for this phenomenon. Of course, it is foolish to drink everyday wines out of crystal, so, because shapes are standardized, I suggest you buy identical glasses of varying quality.

GLASS SHAPES

Red Burgundy
or Bordeaux

Sherry Copita

Rhine Hock

Champagne

Alsace
(green stem)

Tulip All-Purpose
white, red or Champagne

One other imperative is that the glass be perfectly clear, uncut and uncolored. Anything else would interfere with your judgment of the wine's appearance. A century ago tinted glasses were in vogue. They served a purpose then. They obscured a view of wines which were imperfectly filtered and, therefore, cloudy.

In pouring the wine, angle the glass and let the liquid flow gently down the side. Cascades are lovely at Victoria Falls, but wine should throw no spray. The most fastidious oenophiles will actually spill out the first few drops. This carries away any dust or cork crumbs that may have gathered in the bottle's neck.

THE ART OF TASTING

Visual

The color of a wine is always judged against what you expect it to be. An old Burgundy or Port will predictably be tawny, but a Chablis, never. Judging is a matter of experience. Appearance, on the other hand, must conform to more obvious and logical criteria. The principal thing to notice is whether the wine looks "healthy." We'll slide past the exact definition of that word for the moment, but in essence it is the total of all your visual observations. If the wine fails in any way it is less than healthy. The surface of the wine should shine. If it is dull or cloudy, it is flawed. The single exception might be a fine red wine which may have been roughed up enough to mix the sediment back up into the wine. This would be your fault, not the winemaker's. It will settle back in time. A natural and undesired cloudiness is the result of some microbiological evolution or mishandling. A healthy color (called "robe") is clean and sparkling.

Next, look through the wine and check the depth of color. The wine should always be played against a white background; anything else would obviously distort the color. Natural light is best for judging wines. My living room is awful. The walls are all green felt and I am forced to carry my glass into our white bathroom. My uptown friends are amused; I try not to think about it. The depth of the color helps indicate the origin and type of wine. Fine young French red wines tend toward purple (especially Burgundies), while Californias seem to be only deep red. Moselles are pale and greenish, while their cousins the Rhines are more straw and steely. This is, of course, confounded by wines changing color in aging, but it is still a good hint. The intensity or density of color, particularly in red wines, is an indication of the taste intensity and style of the wine. A bright red color can mean a wine of high acidity. A washed out, thin, or orange tint will usually be the sign of a rainy year or nasty vinification. Color also tells the age of a wine, but we'll get further into that in a later chapter.

REDS

Purple →	Ruby →	Red →	Red Brown →	
Extreme	*Threshold*	*Ready*	*Slight Oxidation*	
Youth	*Maturity*		*Nicely Mature*	

Mahogany →	Tawny →	Amber Brown
Mellow and	*In Port—OK*	*Too Old*
Ageing	*In Wine—Dying*	
Bordeaux—15 yrs		
Burgundy—10 yrs		

ROSES

Gris →	Onion skin →	Partridge Eye →	Pink →
Rose Grey from	*Provence—*	*Burgundy,*	*Light*
Anjou, Lorraine	*Tawny Pink*	*Sparkling Topaz*	*Rose*
or Algeria—			*Loire*
Never U.S.			

Orange →	Blue Tinge
Tavel	*Poor Quality*
Full Bodied	

WHITES

Pale Yellow Green →	Straw Yellow →	Gold Yellow →	Gold →
Most Light-Bodied	*Fresh Young*	*Heavier or*	*Well-Aged*
Young Wines	*Wine*	*Sweeter*	*Dry Wine or*
High Acidity			*Rich Botretised*
			Wine

Old Gold →	Yellow Brown →	Amber Brown →	Maderized Brown
Fully Aged	*Feeble*	*Dying*	*Dead*
OK for Big Wine			
Bad for Light Wine			

There is one other thing to check visually: the "legs" of the wine. Swirl the glass so the wine runs up the sides, then let it come to rest. Colorless, oily beads will form and flow down the glass like raindrops down a window. This is the wine's glycerin and alcohol at work (which are related to sugar), one measure of the wine's body. Its presence or absence should be judged in relation to the type of wine. Little would be expected in a rosé, which is exceedingly light, of course, but the great sweet dessert wines and the full-bodied reds should show it clearly.

Smell

Some wine pedants like to break up the act of wine tasting into sight, swirl, smell, sip and savor. I think such alliteration is a continuous conceit covering a common continuance of occurrences.

Next is the olfactory assessment. As noted earlier, your glass should be less than one-third full. You don't need much wine for judging it, because tasting is not drinking. The swirling of the wine increases its surface contact with the air and vaporizes the aldehydes and esters. Logically this accentuates the smell. It is a natural process to grip the glass by the base and sniff the vapors. There are two things to detect. First there is *aroma*—the basic grape, fruit or flower smells that are so much the appeal of a young wine. *Bouquet*, on the other hand, develops only with age. It is mellow and complex, and owes its development to the wood it was aged in and to subtle, time-consuming interactions.

There is a third level of smells as well: these are chemical and negative. It's not uncommon to be able to detect sulfur dioxide in white wines, or hydrogen sulfide or ethyl acetate, all of which will bring you no joy. Many "off" odors will quickly dissipate upon exposure to air. In addition there is a common occurrence—especially in old red wines—categorically referred to as "bottle stink," when malodorous vapors gather in the bottle neck once you've pulled the cork. Ignore them for ten minutes and they should start to go away. Time cures many faults.

What is an off color? Damp socks, I suppose, burnt matches or fusel oil or any swamp-like odor: anything that seems wrong and unnatural. Acquired bouquet, on the other hand, would remind one of fine cigars in old cigar boxes, the woody smell of an old attic, of cool moss or some such thing. At the risk of creating a pseudopalindrome: good smells smell good.

Describing the wine means describing its attributes. There are the general phrases, such as power or intensity, hardness or smoothness, complexity or simplicity. These speak of the over-all characteristics of the wine. Second, there are specific descriptors in both the organic (fruity, flinty, flowery) and the chemical (tannin, acid, maderization) areas. Over time you will refine your own vocabulary. Wine must always be tasted slowly, with almost religious deliberation, in order to permit the concentration necessary to analyze the various sensations. Delay in swallowing accentuates subtleties.

Taste

Since the two senses are so closely allied, the same approach used in assessing the bouquet can be applied to tasting the wine itself. Tasting a wine is similar to sniffing it, but adds the dimension of time. There are three separate stages in taste: initial impression, taste, and after-taste.

Initial impression is the wine's first effect on the palate and mouth. It includes recognition of the basic characteristics of sweetness, bitterness or acidity. Taste comes next. Sip a little wine and breathe in through your mouth as a grandmother with a spoon of hot soup would do. It is at this point that the real complexity of the wine should become apparent to you. After-taste is more than just a memory of the wine; it is how well its components blend together.

That is the time framework, but the actual composition of the taste will be made up of judgments as to the sweetness, flavor (organic), body, and balance (texture) of the wine. Always look for the balance and appropriateness of the taste. The high amount of residual sugar necessary for a Sauternes would be a blunder in a Soave. The grape and style of the wine—not the absolute amount of any single component—will determine what the wine should taste like. For example, Italian red wines traditionally have more of a harsh bite, while red Burgundies, because of the Pinot Noir grape, are notably softer and more velvety.

The most obvious element of taste is sweetness versus dryness. That is an observation. The judgment is whether the amount present is appropriate for the type of wine and if it is balanced by the proper amount of acidity. Too much acid and the wine would bite unpleasantly, too little and it is lopsidedly flabby. Similarly, a wine may be harsh or smooth. Either can be correct depending on the context. A young Piedmont red wine will be harsh but will mellow with age. A Beaujolais, at first, is soft. Softness is something that beginning wine drinkers are usually drawn to. It has an immediacy of appeal and is associated with fruity wines. It also generally means the wine will lack character and will not improve with age. Harshness in the extreme is no virtue either; it is only considered desirable where it indicates that the wine will mature and develop into something more interesting. Harshness is a function of tannin and alcohol, both of which are aggressive tastes.

Alcohol comes into play again in measuring body. "Body" is the weight or density (of sensation) of wine in the mouth, and this feeling of presence is in proportion to the alcohol present. If the idea of body confuses you, think of milk. It is very heavy-bodied. High-alcohol wines (14%) are said to be chewy, full of flavor: Châteauneuf-du-Pape or Hermitage are two such wines. They especially come from southern regions which receive a lot of sun. As you will continue to notice, sun means sugar, sugar means alcohol and alcohol means color and body. Light-bodied wines (9% alcohol) come from the northern wine limits, most noticeably the Rhine and Moselle, and have a delicacy that cannot be present in a robust wine. Northern wines also run heavily toward acidity and are more vulnerable to being out of balance in years without sufficient sun to produce sugar.

Now we come to the term "flavor," which is the combination of aroma, bouquet and taste. It is the flavor of the wine that combines all your reactions. The amount of flavor, from tasteless to full, is an important summation.

Last, there is the "finish," what remains with you after you have swallowed the wine. In a correctly made wine, one should be left with a feeling of harmony, lingering fruit, just the right amount of acid and perhaps a nicely textured velvety impression. Probably more than even bouquet or taste, it is the duration of the after-taste that is the hallmark of a fine wine. It should linger, complex and indefinable, like the fading notes of a symphony.

As in many other explanations, we've gone into exaggerated detail. Several pages have been used to dissect an action that won't take you half a minute to perform. This unfortunately gives a misleading impression of formality. Try to keep your reactions relaxed and spontaneous, and don't give the whole performance more gravity than it merits.

Most professionals impose on themselves a rigid form of grading wines in order to objectify their responses. The Department of Enology of the University of California at Davis uses a system that allocates points according to each major category. I do not see that it is particularly applicable to those outside the trade. It is another discipline that stands between you and your pleasure. It has one usefulness, however, and that is to see how much weight serious students give each component.

		perfect scores
(1)	Clarity and freedom from sediment	2
(2)	Color (depth and tint and appropriateness, for type)	2
(3)	Aroma and bouquet	4
(4)	Freedom from acetic odor	2
(5)	Total acid to the taste	2
(6)	Tannin (astringency)	2
(7)	Extract (body)	1
(8)	Sugar	1
(9)	General flavor	2
(10)	Over-all impression	2
		20

Before passing on to the next chapter I would like to add my bit to the superfluity of writings on wine storage. Heat and temperature fluctuation can destroy a wine in time. The ideal temperature is approximately 55°F. Not all wines react in the same way. Red wines are hardier than whites, and wines that are high in alcohol are more stable than light wines. Chemical variations make certain wines less prone to deterioration than others, but all wines are hurt if the temperature is in excess of 75°F. Temperature *stability* is also important, since changes fatigue and can ruin wine.

This myth of vulnerability can be overstated; incipient oenophiles quiver over their gallons of Gallo on every warm day. It only has an effect on wines that are going to be laid down for years. If you are storing a few cases for a year or two, nothing much will happen, unless you put them on a heater or in a freezer. We stabilize the temperature around us for our own comfort; within these limits the wine is safe. There is, of course, always an exception. Twenty-year-old Burgundies are very fragile, and prolonged exposure would definitely harm them. Young wine, however, will not suffer significantly from a limited life in the 70s or even a brief excursion into the 80s. But be prudent! Keep your wine in the dark, in the back of a closet, under a bed or anywhere the temperature is stable.

In the case of premium wines, there is a crude formula you can use. *For every increase of 10°F., you double the maturation rate.* A wine stored at 75°F. will be ready four times as fast as one at 55°F. This is a handy but crude formula. So if you want to put down a treasure for a decade of aging, you have to find a temperature-controlled public warehouse. Most big cities have at least one, and they are safer than trusting friends with a cellar. Remember: You want your wine untouched.

There is one other alternative, one that all of us contemplate from time to time, and that is the possibility of temperature controlling a closet. The neatest way to do it is to buy one of the three or four commercial self-contained wine storage units. These are large, refrigerated boxes with perfect temperature control. Their prices will remind you that brigandry isn't dead. Prices can exceed ten dollars per bottle stored, two thousand bucks for a two-hundred-bottle unit. Since my royalty payments are mailed and don't come in a Brinks truck, I have yet to indulge in one.

Instead, I built one myself. It is ugly, flimsy, and probably inefficiently insulated. It was also inexpensive. It holds up to 325 bottles and cost me $200, but I admit to shamefully underpaying a friend who is a carpenter. I rationalized that a refrigerator maintains a constant temperature well below that which is necessary for wine so I could therefore cool a larger area with the same unit, but at a higher temperature. I pirated the cooling unit from an abandoned refrigerator. I flattened out the freezer, built a large insulated box with shelves, and affixed the now-flat freezing unit to the inside top. The heat transfer unit is on the bottom, aided by a small fan connected in a series. Below the freezing unit, I have a pan to catch condensed moisture. I also bought a special thermostat that is accurate within 2°F. that works on the air. The wine itself, being 800 times denser, maintains a more constant temperature. I keep it set at 60°F., and it has worked flawlessly for years.

Another factor to keep in mind is allowing new wines to rest. Personal experience brought this home quite clearly to me. I purchased a case of old Rioja wines, waited a few days, and tried one. Awful. I didn't have the heart to serve it to guests, and was not about to have it myself. It languished in the corner, forgotten or avoided for three months, until with the shrug of resignation that I usually reserve for turnips served to me at a friend's house, I chose it one night to accompany some heavy stew dish. It was wonderful. The few bottles I still have are among my favorites. Could I have gotten the one bad bottle in the case? Sure, but the probability of that is .0825, and the same thing has happened on too many other occasions. So if you buy an interesting wine, even one as sturdy as a three-year-old Chardonnay, but which you know has recently been shipped, lay it down for a few months. No one knows why, but the traveling traumatizes it.

RATING GUIDE AND PEAK PERIODS FOR SPECIFIC TYPES OF WINES

	Red Burgundy	White Burgundy	Red Bordeaux	White Bordeaux	Sauternes	Beau-jolais	Red Rhône	Alsace	Rhine	Moselle
1959	18 73-76	17 VG	17 73-79	16 VG	17 73-76	17	17 VG	18 VG	19 VG	20 VG
1960	7 NE	12 NE	13 73-76	12 NE	5 NE	10	17 VG	12 NE	5 NE	5 NE
1961	20 73-80	19 73-76	20 73-80's	19 73-75	19 73-77	18	19 73-75	17 VG	16 NE	17 NE
1962	16 75-78	16 73-75	16 73-77	16 73-75	18 73-76	16	16 73-75	16 VG	13 NE	12 NE
1963	8 NE	10 NE	8 NE	6 NE	4 NE	9	8 NE	10 NE	11 NE	10 NE
1964	17 75-78	17 73-75	15 73-78	12 NE	6 NE	16 VG	16 73-78	15 VG	17 73-75	18 73-78
1965	8 NE	9 NE	9 NE	10 NE	4 NE	10	13 VG	9 NE	5 NE	5 NE
1966	17 75-80's	16 73-75	18 74-80	10 NE	10 NE	17 VG	17 73-77	14 73-74	17 73-75	16 73-75
1967	13 75-80	14 73-75	16 74-78	16 73-74	18 73-75	18 VG	16 73-78	18 73-75	18 73-80	17 73-77
1968	5 NE	12 NE	7 NE	13 73-74	8 NE	11 NE	6 NE	8 NE	8 NE	7 NE
1969	20 74-80's	18 73-80	13 74-80	16 73-76	15 73-80	18 73-74	16 74-80	15 73-75	17 73-80	17 73-80
1970	18 73-80	19 74-80	18 76-80's	18 74-80's	19 75-80's	18 73-75	20 75-80's	16 73-76	15 73-76	15 73-76
1971	19 76-80	19 74-80	17 75-80's	17 74-80's	16 76-80's	16 73-75	18 76-80's	19 73-78	20 75-80's	20 75-80's
1972	16 78-82	13 78-80	12 78-84	13 78-80	11 78-80	13 VG	14 78-84	11 78-80	13 78-80	14 78-80
1973	17 78-82	17 78-82	16 79-80's	14 78-80	13 78-82	14	14 78-82	15 78-82	17 78-84	17 78-84
1974	14 78-80	15 78-80	13 79-84	14 78-80	11 78-82	12 78-79	14 78-82	15 78-82	13 78-80	13 78-80
1975	12 79-80	15 79-81	19 80-90's	16 80's	19 80-90	11 NE	16 79-85	16 79-82	18 80-90's	18 80-90's
1976	19 80's	18 79-84	14 80's	13 79-82	14 79-85	19 79-81	16 79-85	19 79-84	20 80-90's	20 80-90's

Rating Scale: From a low of 1 to the highest quality at 20.
NE—Now if Ever: Poor year with little lasting power.
VG—Only the Very Great are still drinkable—but better than NE.

III

CHEMICAL
COMPONENTS

Very few of us have sufficient self-discipline when it comes to pleasure. We want to start in the high country of Grand Cru wines without ever having served our apprenticeship learning the basics. Nonetheless, it is necessary first to learn what makes up a wine. Until we recognize the relationships among the basic component tastes, we will never understand the whole wine.

When you hear a person describing a wine, the phrases he uses will ultimately be based on the actual chemical composition of the wine. The image of wine may be glamorous, but the knowledge is founded on mundane facts. It would therefore now be wise to get acquainted with the influence that the most prominent chemicals and compounds have on the taste of the wine. Some of the important ones, such as alcohol or water, are immediately familiar. One does not add water to wine to learn the taste of water; instead, it helps to show the diluted taste one can expect from a rainy vintage. If an expert says that a wine has "body," he mainly means that it has a high alcoholic content. Conversely, a "light" wine has little alcohol. It is the same as in painting or any other art form. The more you are able to recognize the subtleties of a wine, the better position you will be in to appreciate it.

Chemistry provides the background of a wine, but is itself not the normal province of the wine buff. However, since so many tastes in wine are directly linked to or influenced by chemicals, a review of the basic chemical components is invaluable. No Faustian oenologist has yet been able to break apart and identify the thousands of constituents in a glass of wine, though the major ones are known as well as many minor ones.

The pleasure of wine is in its taste and its bouquet. We use our very acute senses of smell and taste to analyze what we are consuming. It is easy for us to recognize the basic tastes of sweet, sour (acid), salty and bitter; we will need only a few simple tastings in order to learn to associate these tastes to their primary cause in wine. Together with mental concentration, this process of familiarization is the key to maximum sensitivity of the palate. Man is a subjective animal, yet what we are trying to construct here is a rational method of tasting.

We sense wine mostly either by smell or taste. In order to smell a substance it must be volatile. This means it must vaporize enough to permit some of its molecules to travel through the air. The molecules are inhaled to a tiny, three-sixteenth-square-inch area in the upper rear of the nose, where the necessary chemical reactions occur. The smell is analyzed, electrochemically coded, and passed on to the brain for recognition.

Some substances like salt are non-volatile, so we cannot smell them. Other substances such as vanilla actually have no taste, but are *only* perceived by smell. You don't taste the vanilla in vanilla ice cream, you only smell it.

Warm substances are more volatile than cold ones. That is why a warm wine has more bouquet. A wine taster will hold the wine in his mouth a few seconds before swallowing, to aid the volatile substances in rising up the rear nasal passages.

Our ability to taste is extremely limited. It allows us to identify only four dimensions—sweet, sour, salty or bitter—and to evaluate their relative concentrations. In many cases the tongue cannot differentiate between members of the same stimulus group. Two acids (such as nitric and acetic) would taste basically the same to us, and can only be distinguished by their odors.

The main *sweet* tastes we will encounter in wine are primarily due to glycerin, alcohol and sugar (glucose). Most *bitter* tastes are phenolic compounds (don't let these chemical terms throw you) derived from the grapes before and during fermentation. Wines high in tannin also generally rate high on the bitterness scale. *Salt* is unlikely to occur but can sometimes be detected in certain Spanish sherries or Portuguese red wines which are aged near the sea. *Acids*, on the other hand, are quite common. The principal ones are tartaric acid, malic acid, lactic acid, and tannic acid.

In addition, we can distinguish certain chemical substances by the way we perceive them. Alcohol will leave a burning taste. Tannin will be astringent and perhaps bitter like overbrewed tea. And iron, of course, will be metallic.

Wine contains a multitude of odors. We learn to recognize them by isolating the main ones, or by increasing their presence to the point where they mask the others. The best tasting method is paired comparison. Take two glasses of a simple California red jug wine and add to one glass a small quantity of the component in which we are interested. The unadulterated glass is called the control sample, the other the "doctored" wine. By comparing the taste of the two, the adulteration should be thrown into sharp relief. If you want to play an even more subtle game, you can start by adding only minute quantities of the chemical and increasing the dosage until you first can detect it. That way you discover and sharpen your threshold of perception.

Any chemical we add to a wine already exists in it. What we are doing is intensifying its presence. By strengthening it we taste it in a natural environment. It can also be argued that since you want to familiarize yourself with just the tastes, it would be better to combine them with distilled water instead of wine. It is your choice; either method is acceptable.

The chemicals or compounds you are going to taste fall into two categories: those readily available, such as water, alcohol or sulfur dioxide, and those that must be bought from a pharmacist, such as tannin or glycerin. In any case, these chemicals are the same ones you will find in varying quantities in every glass of wine. Almost all naturally come from the grape itself or are formed as a by-product of fermentation. These would include water, alcohol, tannin, etc. Only a few, and those are usually the off odors, come about because the vintner did something wrong, or added something that doesn't belong. Except where noted, you can feel safe that most of the taste you get came straight from the grape and not from someone's chemical miscalculation.

WATER. The reason for adding bottled (chlorine free) water to wine is to notice how it dilutes the taste. Rain just before harvest will have a similar effect. Since a major part of the enjoyment of wine is its concentration of taste, a watery or thin wine is less pleasant.

Dosage: ¼ tablespoon per 8-ounce glass
Source: Home

ALCOHOL. There are many types of alcohol. The one that is associated with wine is ethyl alcohol. It is difficult to purchase ethyl alcohol, so an excellent substitute is vodka. Like pure alcohol, vodka is essentially odorless and tasteless. The percentage of alcohol in a wine can be an indication of quality. Alcoholic strength is also closely tied to body. The more there is, the more substantial or weighty a wine will feel. Even though alcohol has no taste, it still has a feeling. It leaves a burning sensation.

> Dosage: ½ tablespoon per 8-ounce glass
> Source: Home

TANNIN. Tannin is the chemical that flavors and to some extent preserves wine. It comes from the skin, from the grape pip and from the wood the wine is aged in. Since most of the tannin in a wine comes from the seeds and skins, a red wine will contain two or three times as much tannin as a white. The amount of tannin present will vary. Some grapes, such as the Cabernet Sauvignon used in Bordeaux wines, are very high in tannin. Others are modestly low. Tannin is very astringent, like over-brewed tea. It allows a wine to age, but its bitterness makes young wine less palatable. Over a period of time, the tannin level will decrease and the full flavor of the wine comes forth. The presence of tannin is therefore an indication of a young wine. Tannin may also be present in very old wines. Wines with too much tannin never really age properly. Still, tannic bitterness is a clear hint of youth.

Grape tannin is difficult to obtain. Wood tannin is available from a pharmacist. Wood tannin has a more astringent taste and a bit of a woody aroma.

> Dosage: ¼ tablespoon per 8-ounce glass
> Source: Pharmacy

VOLATILE ACIDITY. Acids are very necessary for wine. Without acid to balance sugar, a wine would be flabby and characterless. But the acid must be the right type. The main volatile (smellable) acid you will run into is acetic acid, which is the sour component of vinegar. Its pungent sour smell and prickly acid taste are clear signs of a wine which has been attacked by acetic acid-producing bacteria and has been spoiled. The bacteria which cause this are carried in the air and so you find this when there has been exposure to oxygen.

Dosage: 1 tablespoon per 8-ounce glass
Source: Home—*wine* vinegar

FIXED ACIDITY. Fixed acids are not readily vaporized by heat, so it is difficult to smell them. The two most important fixed acids are tartaric and malic acids. Malic acid is quite assertive and if the young wine is high in acidity, the vintner will encourage it to undergo malo-lactic fermentation where the malic acid is converted to the less assertive and softer lactic acid. The causes and control of this malo-lactic fermentation are not well understood by wine chemists. Not infrequently, a newly bottled wine will start fermenting again. So, if you happen across a bottle of lightly sparkling wine which is meant to be still, most likely this was caused by the secondary fermentation.

Dosage: Not inducible by simple home methods

Tartaric acid is the major "sour" acid you taste in wine. It is the one that seems to eat holes in your tongue. It is most strongly present in young wines, and precipitates out as small crystals of cream of tartar which may be white in white wines or reddish/purple in red wines. Time and temperature cause it to solidify out of the alcohol—the lower the temperature, the more the precipitation. Sometimes when you draw the cork from a bottle you will notice tiny diamond-like crystals adhering to the underside of the cork. That is cream of tartar. Instead of on the cork, it might just fall as part of the deposit to the bottom of the bottle. It is a natural process and seldom means a fault in the wine. The exception is when the wine was stored in some place that was too cold, which might have had other effects on the wine.

Dosage: ¼ tablespoon per 8-ounce glass
Source: Pharmacy—cream of tartar

GLYCERIN. Glycerin is a colorless, odorless, viscous liquid of sweetish taste, though less sweet than sugar. When we talk about richness in a wine it would usually mean, among other things, a high level of glycerin. The glycerin content is mainly dependent on the ripeness of the grape. Super-ripe grapes, ones used in the great dessert wines of Sauternes, the Rhine, Moselle and Tokay, have disproportionately high levels of glycerin caused as a by-product of the noble rot, Botrytis Cinerea. Because of glycerin's oily nature, it is common to think of it in connection with the "legs" of a wine, but the legs are actually caused by alcohol. The legs are the tearlike streaks that are formed on the inside of a glass as you swirl the wine. Glycerin is as much a texture term as one of taste. When a wine is described as thick, oily or viscous, glycerin will be a main cause.

Dosage: ¼ tablespoon per 8 ounces wine
Source: Pharmacy

SUGAR (Sucrose). Another source of sweetness in wine will, of course, be its sugar content. At the right levels, some sweetness will aid in your perception of the component tastes of the wine. Beyond that, it masks flavors and is used to hide off-tastes in poor wine. Try it at different concentrations in a dry wine to see how it affects your perceptions.

Dosage: Variable
Source: Home—confectioners

SULFUR DIOXIDE. The gas, sulfur dioxide, is added primarily to white wines to inhibit harmful organisms and allow beneficial yeasts to ferment the wine. The main arvantage of SO_2 is in keeping white wines white. It used to be a frequent complaint that because of the over-zealous use of sulfur dioxide, the white wines of the Graves region had a sulfur smell. This is something you may still encounter from time to time in white wines. When it occurs, fortunately, the smell will dissipate after the bottle has been opened and the wine has been permitted to breathe. Sulfur dioxide is a toxic gas and should not be experimented with. Instead, just think of the smell of a burnt match head. If something like that shows up in a wine's bouquet, ascribe it to sulfur dioxide.

HYDROGEN SULFIDE. The rotten egg smell that is occasionally encountered is caused by hydrogen sulfide. It is the fault of bad vineyard practices, negative yeast strains, or, more commonly, lack of proper care in the winery. If, too near harvest time, sulfur is sprayed on the vines, the residue will form hydrogen sulfide during fermentation. This can still be prevented by a good winemaker by letting the sulfur residue fall out of the white juice or by centrifuging the wine. In France it is illegal to spray with sulfur after the first of August. Hydrogen sulfide may also come from the dripping of the sulfur candles that are used to sterilize the wooden barrels prior to storing the wine. Like rotten eggs, it is too unpleasant to warrant a tasting.

METHYL ANTHRANILATE. There is a "foxy" aroma to Concord (native American) grapes. It is a taste that is unknown to wines made from vines originating in Europe. It is caused by methyl anthranilate, and it takes some getting used to by people who were raised on California or Continental wine. Most New York State wines come from Concord or the related Vitis Labrusca grapes, so the taste is quite noticeable. It has some relationship to bubble gum or, if you've ever run into it, that dire Peruvian drink Inca Cola. Actually, the amount of methyl anthranilate is controlled by something called the Tressler Method. Sparkling New York State wines are frequently blended to control anthranilate levels.

Dosage: 300 PPM*
Source: Chemical supply house

ISOAMYL ALCOHOL. One of the odorous constituents that impart a yeasty aroma to wine is isoamyl alcohol. Its presence adds character and flavor to red wines and brandy. It is also a fusel oil, and if it is present in too high a quantity it can give you a headache.

Dosage: 300 PPM
Source: Wine chemical supply house

ACETALDEHYDE. There are only minimal amounts of acetaldehyde present in most newly fermented wine. Over time, as components of the wine oxidize (combine with oxygen), its presence greatly increases. It imparts a sharp, "faded" odor to a wine which has started to turn brown. In certain cases, it is very beneficial. Acetaldehyde produced by flor sherry yeasts give Fino and Amontillado sherries their unique flavor.

Dosage: 300 PPM
Source: Wine chemical supply house

Further tastings can include 2-phenethyl alcohol, which is produced by yeast fermentation and has a cheap perfume-like smell. Its main function seems to be in low concentration as a carrier of other component odors.

There are two other chemistry-based expressions you will frequently encounter. They are *oxidation* and *maderization*, and neither requires the addition of any chemicals to the wine.

---

* Parts per million.

OXIDATION. Oxidation is one of those lovely nets that people orally throw to cover any spoiled wine. It refers to a deterioration of the wine and is not a specific chemical. As the name implies, it is related to the excessive absorption of oxygen. It spoils a wine by robbing it of its freshness. It renders the flavor and the color dull. White wines become tawny while red wines become brown. It is usually caused by a faulty cork that lets too much air in, or by the wine being too old. An oxidized wine tastes just plain dead.

It is good to learn to recognize an oxidized wine. All you have to do is let some open wine sit out for a day or two. Hopefully, no meaningful amount of vinegar will form in that time and the flat dull taste you get will be due to oxidation alone.

MADERIZATION. Maderization is another very common term and even experts seem to confuse it with oxidation. It usually occurs when a wine is stored in too warm a place. The result is a slightly burnt sherry- or Madeira-like smell, and the wine again loses its freshness.

To get to recognize it, all you have to do is take a little leftover wine, keep it in the bottle, but leave it near a radiator or put it in a very slow oven (130°F.) for a day or two.

In most cases, maderization is a fault, but in the case of Madeira wine, this heating is closely controlled, taking up to six months, and the results are very pleasing.

A rigorous wine-appreciation course under the sponsorship of the University of California is given several weekends a year at Lake Arrowhead. In much the same manner as described here, it trains the palate to be objective. If you are interested, write Dr. A. D. Webb, Chairman, Department of Viticulture & Enology, University of California, Davis, CA 95616.

Many of these chemical components such as tartaric acid, tannic acid, citric acid, glycerin and (montrachet) yeast are available from Miccio Laboratories. The prices average $1.75 each for a minimum quantity of 4 ounces. A complete brochure is available upon request. Miccio Laboratories: 57 Spring Street, New York City 10012.

IV

ATTRIBUTES

Experience makes the difference between the beginner and the expert. There is an underlying trick to learning to taste wines, however, and that is to form a basis from which to judge them. Most people try a Chianti on Monday, say, and next have a Portuguese green wine with Friday's dinner. Then they soon become frustrated when they can't learn anything about wine. Wine remains a mystery to them because they don't approach it properly.

The interest of wine is in its diversity. Wines vary in taste because they are made from different varieties of grapes. Once you know the basic taste of each *grape*, you can compare different vintages (different harvests) of the same wine in order to understand the effect of variables like weather and age. Two different years may be excellent, but the wines will be different—variations on the same theme. Because the weather is quite different from year to year, the vintage year of a wine becomes very important.

The next stage is to learn how *age* affects wine—how time improves it or makes it deteriorate. You can learn how age mellows a fine wine by tasting a younger bottle versus an older one.

The effect of *weather* is studied next. This is done by comparing the same wine in two different vintages. Climate affects the acidity, color, and ripeness of the grapes.

Temperature affects the acid-alcohol balance.

Soil affects their chemical composition. You can learn this by comparing two wines of the same type grown in different soils or climates and noting how they differ.

When you combine all of these, you get the dominant, natural influences on the final taste of the wine, and on its *color*.

This is, of course, simplistic. Obviously, the taste of wine is affected by more things than just age, weather, temperature, soil or grape type. It is also the product of the skill and style of the man who made it, and the way it has been handled since it was bottled. Each of the attributes common to all wine can be brought into sharp focus for the enthusiast to recognize and learn. Armed with this background, the enthusiast has the basis on which to judge whether a wine is sound or unsound and just how fine it is.

THE GRAPE

The beginning of a wine is the grape, and the beginning of its taste is the taste of that grape. There are 25,000 varieties of grapes, not counting the hybrids, crossbreeds and miscellaneous progeny developed by the "mad scientists" at the Universities of Davis, Geisenheim, and Bordeaux. Fortunately, few are utilized for wine consumption, or we would be besieged by more models than a GM dealer can display on a discount Tuesday.

Man has been drinking wine for thousands of years, but it is probable that an extinct race of birds was the first to find that wine has more than nutritional benefits. Overripe grapes ferment, and the birds that quickly came to appreciate this fact would have ended up flopping around drunk on their backs, easy prey for any enemies. Man had no more self-control, only more discernment. He chose the grapes he liked and turned those into wine, convincing his brethren both of the beneficial release of intoxication and the superior quality of his particular brew. Snobbery was born early.

Not all grapes make good wine. In fact, very few do. Perhaps twenty varieties make up ninety-five percent of the wine we consume, and four of these types shine brighter than the North Star. Alone, these four varieties are responsible for the great wines of Champagne, Burgundy, Bordeaux, the Rhine and Moselle, as well as the best wines of California and New York. They do not hold a patent on greatness, but their con-

sistent excellence and widespread use makes them stand out above
the others. These grapes are termed "noble grapes." They are:

- Cabernet Sauvignon
- Pinot Noir
- Chardonnay (incorrectly called Pinot Chardonnay)
- Riesling

There are other varieties that are also sometimes called noble. The term
is loosely applied to any grape that produces a wine of exceptional
quality, complexity and breed. The Hungarian Tokay-Furmint grape
is a noble grape when grown in Hungary. The great Nebbiolo of Northern Italy is another, while the Merlot, which is the dominant grape of
St. Emilion and Pomerol, is a third. But these grapes, though great,
tend to be limited in production and restricted to only a few areas. If
they were more widely distributed and grew as well elsewhere, perhaps
they would be more appreciated.

Another class of grapes produces superb wines, with only a touch less
glory to them than the nobles possess. They bear more fruit, are more
widely grown, and vary more in quality. They produce wines that are
appreciated rather than studied, charming rather than distinguished.

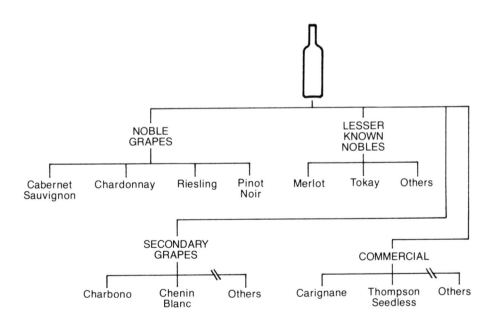

These grapes make most of the table wines we consume, and their quality is normally excellent. When well made (which is the norm), the wine may be delicate and refreshing, or robust and complex—everything one could want from a wine. The Gamay grape is a case in point. It is a prolific and therefore profitable grape, producing appealing if not spectacular wines except in Haut- and Bas-Beaujolais. There it flowers into the Beaujolais wine which is so appealing. Another is the Chenin Blanc grape, which gives us the soft, fruity wines of the Loire Valley and some wonderful, if expensive, wines in California. Zinfandel is a grape now unique to our West Coast. In youth it is delightful—the Beaujolais of America—and is the backbone of our best jug wine. Well grown, and with age, it becomes a full complex wine similar in style to the famous wines of Bordeaux.

There is a third level of grapes that have names which the consumer seldom sees. They are Thompson Seedless, French Colombard, Mission, and the like. These grapes produce a vast quantity of juice but of such uninteresting quality that they are fit mainly for blending into cheap jug wines. In France, the bottle might be labeled Vin Ordinaire, in California Mountain Red, Chablis, Sauternes, or some other meaningless title. There is a simple rule you can follow with American wines: *If the grape is fine enough to be listed on the label then the producer thinks the wine is of superior quality*. If an American wine carries just a place name (e.g., Chablis or Burgundy) then it is a standard blend, drinkable and hopefully enjoyable but with no claim to greatness. A fine wine can only be made from the finest grapes.

One of the most important and difficult points to understand is that fundamentally there are *two* different types of wine: varietal and generic.

Varietal wines are made from just one variety of grapes (e.g., 100% Cabernet Sauvignon) or are a blend of several grape types of which one predominates and sets the style (e.g., 70% Cabernet Sauvignon, 26% Merlot, 4% Petit Verdot). California *premium* wines are mostly varietals. As a rule, you can say that varietal wines are better than generics.

Any wine that lists the grape on the label will be a varietal wine, but then the confusion starts. Any wine that lists its specific vineyard of origin is also a varietal (e.g., Clos de Bèze) but a wine that talks only of a vague general area (e.g., Bordeaux or Pauillac) is considered a *generic*. Perhaps an illustration might help clear this up. A genuine Chablis coming from the Chablis region of France by law must be made exclusively from Chardonnay. Logically, this should be called a varietal, and it is—providing the label lists the specific vineyard. If it just says Chablis, then it is a generic despite the grape content. A California "Chablis" is obviously a generic because it has only a place name. Likewise Gallo Hearty Burgundy or Almaden Mountain Red are generics.

Since Cabernet Sauvignon, Pinot Noir, Chardonnay and the Riesling grapes are the basis of most of the fine wines to which we are exposed, it is wise to learn to recognize them. With a little exposure this becomes easy. Each has its own characteristic bouquet and taste, quickly identifiable and easily learned. Once you memorize these characteristics, you can authoritatively comment on a wine's "pinot nose"—and understand it.

The grape sets the theme for the wine and is the structure within which the taste must work. The wines we like will be dictated by the grapes from which they are made. You like Burgundies because you like the Pinot Noir grape. You will eventually be able to select the wines you expect to like on the basis of your experience with the grape. The knowledge works both ways. Knowing the grape lets you anticipate the taste of a wine, and it allows you to judge the wine in comparison to its peers. It is also advisable, as well as pleasurable, to try wines made from some of the other grapes. It is knowledge that you are bound to pick up over time, but that will be more valuable if known from the start. Memory is a function of exposure. The more often you taste something, the sooner you will recognize it.

Like a good recipe, each chapter of this book should be read through before any tastings are organized. This is because a single wine might serve to illustrate two points. Rather than buy the same wine twice, use it in conjunction with both tastings simultaneously. Cabernet Sauvignon is studied so that you recognize the grape. Since it will most likely be young and tannic, it will also be compared to an old Spanish Rioja to illustrate the progression and refinements of age. If you have the leisure and the money to try the same wine several times, of course, then do so. But if not, try combining tastings. Repetition is the key to memory and learning.

If you want to learn about wine, then you must start by tasting wine made from the four top noble grapes. These make the best and most interesting wines. It is not the *quality* of the wine we are looking for, but its varietal *character*. Varietal character means how well the wine reflects the basic taste of the grape. Depending on where the wine is made, this may be important. For instance, in California the varietal character is stressed, while in Bordeaux or Burgundy the wines are blended toward a more historical taste, one that is like the traditional taste of the region. It is a difference in esthetics. Winemakers may argue passionately for one approach or the other, but both are valid. For our purposes the stress laid on the inherent grape character makes California wines more useful in this section.

Dismiss from your mind any idea you may have that California wines can't match French wines. It's not so, as you will see later in the book. Our jug wines are probably better than what the average Frenchman consumes, and our best premium wines stand side by side with Europe's best. It is fairest to say that the best French wines are grown in France. The best California wines come from California.

The wines I mention in this chapter are of good quality and value, but the accent will be on how well they illustrate the grape's character. Inglenook wines are very reputable and should be available everywhere. Thus, they are the initial choice. As a preferred alternative, I have suggested a higher quality wine. If you are fortunate enough to have a wineshop near you that stocks the second choice, and you are willing to spend a bit more, then I suggest it. You won't learn more about the grape, but you will be tasting a more handcrafted wine and will have a rarer experience.

Cabernet Sauvignon

Cabernet Sauvignon must be the finest red wine grape; it seems to produce excellent wines virtually everywhere. Its most important accomplishment is the great Châteaux of the Médoc: Châteaux Lafite, Mouton, Latour, Margaux, Haut Brion, and the other sixty classified growths that make Bordeaux famous. "Château" in this context means estate, and implies that the wine comes exclusively from grapes grown on the estate.

Actually, none of these wines is 100% Cabernet Sauvignon. Often Merlot, Cabernet Franc, Malbec or Petit Verdot are blended with it. The theory is that Merlot, which is an outstanding and delicate grape in its own right, adds a soft roundness to the wine. The Petit Verdot darkens the color and yields tannin. The Malbec is supple and soft, similar to a Gamay Beaujolais. It is quick to mature and not long lasting. Last, the Cabernet Franc, a higher percentage of which is used than any of the other grapes, is a way of hedging against weather factors. The Cabernet Franc is a consistent grape. It ripens early and is less affected by climatic variations. It is similar in taste, though more vigorous and less sophisticated than the Cabernet Sauvignon. The real function of these other grapes is to complement and accentuate the basic taste of the Cabernet Sauvignon. Excellent wines are made from the Cabernet Sauvignon elsewhere in France, but Bordeaux is its showplace. Transplanted to the United States, it makes the finest red wine California produces, and it is the basis for the quality wines of Chile, Argentina, South Africa, Australia, and other countries where Europeans have immigrated. As pleasant as it is to drink, so too is it hard to grow and handle. Like all of the noble grapes, the vine produces a few small clusters and proportionately little wine. Therefore its wines are expensive. A regular yield of Cabernet Sauvignon, two to three tons per acre, may be one-third the amount of a more prolific variety.

Cabernet Sauvignon is one of the most tannic of the major wines, which is both good and bad. Tannin from the skin and pits preserves the wine, allowing it to age and develop a complex bouquet and subtle taste. But tannin itself tastes astringent, and makes the wine harsh for drinking when young. As the wine ages, the tannin, together with pigments, solidifies in the solution and forms the sediment found in the bottom of older bottles. This is fine if you can wait years for a wine to properly develop into something remarkable, but it makes for a harsh wine when young.

This is not as extreme as it sounds. "Robust" might better be substituted for "harsh." If a bottle is opened an hour or more before consumption, the astringency disappears. This exposure to air is simply forced aging. Not all Bordeaux wines are made the same way. The petit, or "small Châteaux," farms that are not classified as highly as the prestigious growths, do not have as much tannin and are ready to drink as soon as they are marketed. The Grands Châteaux and the finer wines of California should be allowed to mellow ten years or more. This, of course, depends upon the vintage and winemakers' style. California wines often are not fully appreciated because they are drunk too young. The practice in California is to allow the newly pressed grapes to ferment with their skins only five or six days. Consequently, they don't pick up as much tannin as a Bordeaux wine does. For example, Château Mouton leaves its wine "on the skins" up to three weeks. Thus, while California wines would benefit from more bottle age than they usually are afforded, they don't require as much aging as most Bordeaux wines.

A young Carbernet Sauvignon wine will be a dark ruby color with a velvet texture and a strong complex bouquet—musty when first out of the bottle, but quickly and constantly changing thereafter. Depending on the style of the specific winery, the bouquet will have a smell of ripe, sweet berries, but also a mixture of wood smells and complex aromas with a big smooth body that fills the mouth.

TASTING 1: Cabernet Sauvignon

Preferred:	Inglenook Cabernet Sauvignon
	Beaulieu Cabernet Sauvignon
Alternatives:	Charles Krug Cabernet Sauvignon
	Souverain Cabernet Sauvignon
	Christian Brothers Cabernet Sauvignon
More Expensive:	Beaulieu Private Reserve Cabernet Sauvignon
	Inglenook Individual Cask Cabernet Sauvignon
	Robert Mondavi Cabernet Sauvignon
	Simi Cabernet Sauvignon
Vintages:	1973 or later for any of these wines. The Simi can include their exceptional 1972

Consumerism. American wines are made softer than those of Bordeaux, so do not expect as much harshness. Still, younger bottles are to be preferred because they will exaggerate the traits of the Cabernet. Even though the accent here is not on quality but on variety, avoid inexpensive substitutes. The law allows Americans to blend in less expensive alternatives while still calling the wine Cabernet. This dilutes the full taste of the Cabernet.

Pinot Noir

It is an oddity that the same grape should produce one of the finest red wines in the world and also one of the most appreciated whites. In Burgundy, Pinot Noir is king. It is responsible for all the great red wines of the Côte de Nuits from Santenay in the south through Volnay, Pommard, Beaune, Aloxe-Corton, Nuits-St-Georges and to the incomparable wines of Vosne Romanée (Romanée-Conti, La Tâche, La

Grande Rue) and its neighbors Vougeot (Clos de Vougeot), Morey-St-Denis, Gevrey-Chambertin (Le Chambertin) and Fixin. All these towns and their famous vineyards are planted in Pinot Noir. Other less noble grapes are scorned here.

Once, in 1395, when the more prolific grape, the Gamay, was making inroads into the vineyards, the last Duke of Burgundy, Philip the Bold, ordered them all uprooted and replanted with Pinot Noir. To raise Gamay meant to risk death. Wine can be an art, a livelihood, and a passionate religion.

There is a white side, too, to the Pinot Noir. As you know, the color of a wine comes from the pigmentation in the skin of the grape. When a dark-skinned grape is fermented away from the skin it picks up no color and produces a white wine. If, in addition, the second fermentation takes place in the sealed bottle where the gas cannot escape, the result is Champagne. Most French Champagnes are mixtures of Pinot Noir and Chardonnay at a ratio of about four-to-one. The exception is Champagne labeled Blanc de Blancs, which should be made exclusively from the Chardonnay grape.

Pinot Noir is in its glory when planted in France. Once away from Burgundy, it transplants less successfully than does Cabernet Sauvignon. Abroad it produces substantial wines of high quality, but seldom anything that compares with a fine Burgundy. André Tschelistcheff, California's foremost winemaker for many years, considered production of a perfect Pinot Noir in the United States "almost not obtainable." To him, his only great Pinot Noir success was his 1946 Beaulieu—but then he dwells in dreams.

Pinot Noir produces a soft wine compared to the Cabernet Sauvignon, for it contains far less tannin and acid. It can be appreciated when quite young, as little as four years after the harvest. The more northerly, powerful French wines, such as Chambertin, may require a little more time, since they spend two to three years aging in the cask before they are bottled. More years will improve the wine, but by the time a fine Bordeaux is just becoming drinkable, a Burgundy is fully mature.

A Pinot Noir will have a deep red color in youth, moving to brick and brown-orange with age. The bouquet will be quite expressive and powerful with flowers, fruit and, of course, grapes coming through clearly. The taste is immediately appealing. It fills the mouth. The bite is not the astringent one of tannin but more of sharp alcohol. It is a refreshing wine which leaves a lingering memory of taste.

TASTING 2: The Pinot Noir

Preferred: Mondavi (California)
     Aloxe-Corton

Alternatives: Beaune
     Nuits-St-Georges

Premium: Le Corton

Producers: Bouchard, Drouhin, Jadot, Latour, de Villamont—any of
     the better names listed on page 189

Vintages: 1967, 1969, 1970, 1971, 1972, 1973
     1975 and 1976 might be fine but too young

Consumerism. To get the flavor of a real Pinot Noir, it is necessary to go to Burgundies. It has been suggested that the California Pinot Noirs are less successful because of a lower calcium content in the soil. Be that as it may, there is a ripeness and depth to the Burgundies that can be tasted but not easily described. In successful ones it comes on as a velvety texture both soft and full in wines that are preferably six or more years old. In order to best appreciate it I suggest that you indulge yourself with the premium recommendation.

Riesling

Some say the Riesling is an acquired taste; you need only try it once to become an addict. Its Rhine and Moselle wines are a pure joy. They are alternately light and refreshing, tart and sweet. You can smell flowers, fields and fruits in them. But don't let anyone tell you they are naive, simple wines. They start off young and joyful, but year by year the good ones take on a complexity and depth that is unique.

Let us take a hypothetical Riesling grape (though I prefer real ones). If picked on October 6 of a great year it would produce a lovely but simple wine. However, we know a secret so—risking bad weather—we wait another three weeks for the grape to ripen more before picking. By now we are lucky: A few grapes have started to rot. Yes, lucky, because this "noble rot" evaporates water and concentrates the taste to an essence. The grape shrivels like a raisin and yields little juice, but that little bit is so concentrated in flavor that it is luscious. Depending on the state of the grape when it is picked and the degree of selectivity, the wine is called progressively Spätlese (late picked), Auslese

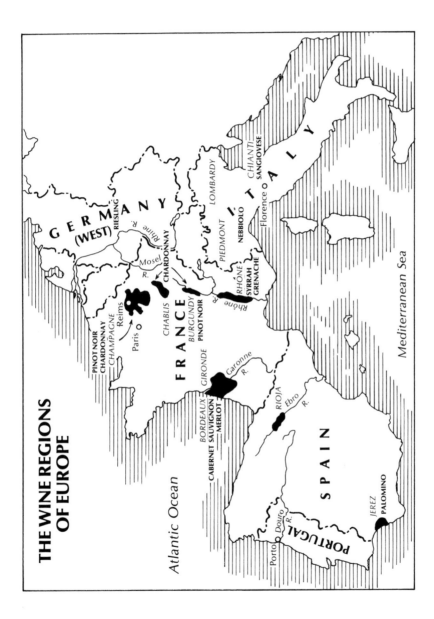

(selected bunches of late-picked grapes), Beerenauslese (selection of individual grapes from bunches) and Trockenbeerenauslese (individually picked dried berries). For this last jawbreaker, it takes two man-days just to gather enough berries for one bottle. The cost is tremendous, but so is the wine. It will last and improve for over half a century.

What makes the Riesling great is that it fights a battle between sweetness and acidity. The soil is acidy and the grape *is* sweet. If either dominated, the wine would be awful, but the presence of the two balancing each other creates a magnificent wine. The sweetness is natural, like perfectly ripe fruit, not cloying like the aftertaste of sugar and water or an artificial dessert. It is like an apple which can be both tart and sweet at the same time.

Admirers of the Riesling carried it to neighboring Alsace, France, and to most other major wine-growing areas. The Riesling in California lacks the zip of acidity and has more alcohol. It is fuller, a bit fat with glycerine, and a different style of wine from the German. Character and body are acquired at the cost of finesse. The Riesling is definitely a cold-climate grape, and the easy life of the California valleys robs it of some of its vitality. But new vineyard areas are constantly being opened and better sites may yet be found. Some small wineries, like Joseph Phelps, are beginning to make interesting wines from Riesling grapes grown in the more rugged mountains. This is one of the areas where the quality in California is changing almost daily.

TASTING 3: Riesling

Preferred:	Piesporter Goldtropfchen Kabinett
Alternatives:	Alsatian Riesling (Dry)
Premium:	Wehlener Sonnenuhr Kabinett (Prumm)
	Graacher Himmelreich Kabinett (Prumm)
Vintages:	1971, 1973, 1975 or 1976
	For a more complete review see page 156

Consumerism. All the recommended wines are from the Moselle region of Germany. They are easily recognized by their green bottles. The wines chosen are all "qualitätswein mit prädikat"—the highest quality level under German law. A simple "qualitätswein" could be used, but the Riesling flavor will not be as concentrated. From the consumer's point of view there is an interesting contradiction here: The wines suggested above may actually cost less, but have a higher level of quality than, the more famous commercial wines like Liebfraumilch, Zeller Schwartz Katz, or Moselblümchen.

Chardonnay

Chardonnay is the elegant grape. It is bone dry and tart, with an undercurrent of flowers. It is all there—but always very subtle. It makes Chablis virginal, Meursault crisp, the Montrachets generous, and gives Blanc de Blancs Champagne finesse. It produces the popular Pouilly-Fuissés. Californians believe that their Chardonnay rivals the greatest wines from France, and they may be right. It doesn't matter if it is a rival. It is enough to say it is a truly fine wine.

While many argue that a Riesling is best drunk alone or with dessert, a Chardonnay goes well with food. Chablis and oysters are famous.* Meursault loves fish, and a Montrachet can match nearly anything capable of competing in such expensive company. The grape name comes from the town of Chardonnay in the Maconnais section of France. It means "place full of thistles," which goes rather aptly with the taste of the wine. This taste seems to vary more than most with the soil in which it is grown, but is always characterized by finesse and piquancy. As with other grapes mentioned, this nobility comes at a cost. Production yield is small, and therefore the wines are expensive.

TASTING 4: Chardonnay

This tasting is very similar to one other later in the book. It would be useful to just look at the recommendations for tasting number 22 which also deals with aspects of the Chardonnay taste. The suggested wines here are just an abbreviated version.

Preferred:	Macon Pinot** Chardonnay
	Robert Mondavi Chardonnay
Alternatives:	Inglenook Chardonnay
	Louis Martini Chardonnay
More Expensive:	Joseph Phelps Chardonnay
	Spring Mountain Chardonnay
	Freemark Abbey Chardonnay

---

* A curious combination, considering Chablis is often referred to as virginal, while oysters are famous for the reverse.
** The word "Pinot" is now usually omitted.

AGE

Wines are alive. They are born, mature, turn senile and die in their own time. They are alive and change because they are a very complex mixture of organic and inorganic compounds, each element of which changes at a different pace. First in the cask and then in the bottle, it is the slow exposure to oxygen that most affects the flavor and the bouquet. This aging is not a consistent process. Wine goes through more fits and changes than a spoiled child. I have known wines to turn around from common to complex in four months. Like children, wines have difficult periods in their development. Bordeaux merchants speak mysteriously of an awkwardness of taste that affects already bottled wines for a week during the flowering and harvesting periods of the vine. I do not know how much substance there is to this form of vine telephathy, but it is true that there are unpredictable short periods when a wine may not be up to its peak.

Older wine, red or white, will taste quite different from the way it tasted in its infant years. It is not true that all red wines should be old, and the older the better. Some wines are meant to be drunk young, some are meant to age. The young wines depend on fruitiness and freshness for their charm; the older wines on complexity, harmony and sophistication brought on over time by the interplay of acids and sugars, esters and aldehydes, pigments and tannins and the constant but slow infusion of oxygen. Aging is very important to wine. When the grape is first pressed, the resulting liquid is cloudy due to particles which are both bitter and visually disturbing. These have to be given a chance to settle down and be "fined" out. The new wine will also be harsh with lingering odors from the yeast. This gives way to aromatic fruitiness and later to bouquet.

An example of a red wine that should be drunk young is Beaujolais. It is illegal in France to sell the Beaujolais Primeur more than six months after it is bottled. Its stronger brother, the Beaujolais Nouveau, is pleasant up to a year, but the fresher the better. Even the strongest Beaujolais, those bearing the town name of Julienas or Morgon and not even labeling itself as Beaujolais, is on shaky legs in four years and flat in eight years. Morgon, Julienas, and Moulin-à-Vent are solid wines which are best following the spring of their vintage. The younger, fast-maturing wines, usually with little color, are drunk as soon as fermenting is complete. Such lesser wines from high up in the hills are drunk in the early autumn. So some red wines, especially the simpler ones, are meant to be drunk young. In fact, most of the world's wines are drunk within a year of their harvest. Out of a total annual production of seven and one-half billion gallons of wine, less than 4 percent is fine enough to warrant aging. Similarly, some white wines are best when they have aged. The simple white wines of the Loire, Portugal and even many from Germany are best when young. A wine with more pretension needs some age to gain balance. Chardonnay or the better Riesling wines need two years to soften and bring together their youthfully awkward tastes. This means a young vintage Champagne (one bearing a date) will not be as pleasant or mellow as its brother that is two to six years older. This is equally true for the white Burgundies (i.e. Meursault, Chassagne-Montrachet, etc.), Chablis (Grand Cru), white Bordeaux, or the estate-bottled German wines. Modern dictum sets ten to twelve years as the age limit of white wines, but this was not always the case, and aged white wines are still popular in many parts of the world. In Argentina they are routinely aged several years and are appreciated with a slight oxidation.

Until World War I, the European taste preferred white wines of ten years minimum age, with a special predilection for old Champagne. In the 1920s, Charles Berry, proprietor of England's most famous wine shop, Berry Brothers & Rudd (a shop so elite it still displays no wine), gave a Champagne dinner, serving 1874 Ruinart, 1919 Perrier-Jouet, 1911 Pol Roger, 1899 and 1906 Veuve Clicquot and 1904 Pommery & Greno. The eldest wines must have been more curious than enjoyable, but in any event, it was an incredible tour de force.

Even today, on occasion, you will come across a thirty-year-old Chablis or fifteen-year-old Bâtard-Montrachet. These are curiosities to be studied, for they illustrate the effects of age on a wine. Young wines are most readily available, and make up the majority of what you drink. But it is important to know what they will eventually become if laid down in your cellar, when they will be at their peak, and precisely what that peak is. You must learn what a wine's potential is and whether it is approaching or leaving it. It would be ideal to taste the same vintage of a particular wine over its entire life span, but that is far from the quickest or most practical method of learning. The best substitute is to compare the same or similar wines over several vintages.

As usual we are at the mercy of the marketplace. Few merchants can be expected to stock supplies of the same wine from many years. It is possible to find older vintages of many wines that simply move slower because of cost or lack of public familiarity. Or, on occasion, a newer vintage will supplant the older one in the bins before the older has sold out.

Another approach is to look for an intrinsically older wine. These are wines whose style requires long cask aging and arrive on the market after ten or more years. Oddly enough, these wines are often underrated and underpriced—ideal for our tastings. They usually come from Northern Italy or Portugal, but the most common are Spain's Rioja Gran Reservas. The main labels are from the Marqués de Riscal, Marqués de Murrieta, Paternina, or Bodegas Bilbainas, and may date 1948, 1949, 1952, 1953, 1955, 1959, 1961, or 1964. The ones from the 1950s are best for our purposes and can still be found for from $4.00 to $8.00. Vintage dates on the label don't tell the whole truth. Not all the wine in the bottle comes from the year listed. The bodegas blend older wines to the style of the vintage year. Most of the wine will be from the label year, but some younger wine may have been added to supplement the body that has been depleted throughout the years of aging. It is an honorable practice meant to produce a sound wine but a bit misleading to the buyer. Nonetheless, the wines are still intrinsically older and therefore useful to us to illustrate age.

The Rioja Reservas, because of the style of wine making, are similar to and an excellent substitute for French clarets at a fraction of the price. The reason lies with the phylloxera, a burrowing louse that began destroying the vineyards of France in the 1870s. French wine growers, faced with ruin, had to move. Spain had not then been affected, so many growers from Bordeaux crossed the Pyrenées and settled in the best wine area, Rioja, on the Ebro River just past the frontier. They brought the French methods and ideals, but unfortunately also brought the louse, which eventually attacked the Spanish vineyards as well.

The Spanish developed a preference for age in their wines. This softens the deep inky colors and strong grape flavors of the Garnacha (related to the Rhône's Grenache) grape. Most Bordeaux châteaux leave their wines in casks two to three years, but Rioja Reserva's may remain in oak as long as ten years. This allows more oxygen to be absorbed by the wine than a corked bottle would permit. Because of this additional oxygen exposure, a Reserva should taste older than a French wine from the same vintage year.

TASTING 5: Recognizing the Effects of Age in Wines

It is instructive to taste a recent Spanish vintage versus a Reserva, since the Reserva's taste of age will be quite apparent. The idea is to show the progression of the wine as age affects it. But time does not affect all wines in the same way. Wine is on a continuum of change, and the only thing we are trying to establish now is the experience of trying one wine in different stages of its career in order to recognize where the basic differences lie. Comparison is always the key, and age is what they have in common. Thus it is only necessary to find virtually *any* wine in a variety of years. The specific type or origin is not crucial, so long as it is the same wine. If it is a blend of different vineyards, such as a Beaujolais, be sure both bottles are from the same bottler, such as Jadot or M. Henri, and—if a specific town is mentioned—that all vintages come from that area or town (e.g., Fleurie, Chénas, Brouilly).

Alternatively, since German wines are often slow movers in a store, you may find two or more vintages from one vineyard. This is especially true since the recent vintages of 1969, 1970, 1971, 1973, 1975 and 1976 have been so successful, and many stores have stocked them. White wines reach maturity more rapidly than reds, so a comparison of years closer together is acceptable. A difference from one year to the next may be noticeable, but two years difference is desirable and four to five even better, though difficult to find. Beaujolais should be approached in the same way since it is a light, early-maturing wine.

Fuller red wines such as Côtes-du-Rhônes, Châteauneuf-du-Pape, Bordeaux, or Northern Italian should have at least four years of separation and, if possible, eight or more. Don't, however, buy a 1955 and 1975 Château Montrose. You'd love it, but the cost would be staggering. Shop around for what is available. General broad changes in taste are more important now than specifics. One thing is critical: Consult the vintage charts in this book and avoid buying disastrous years like 1974 or 1968, in which weather had such an overriding effect that it overwhelmed the other characteristics. All types of adulteration might have been practiced upon the wine in order to save the crop and make the wine more palatable. The end product may be a sound wine but still contain extraneous elements that would interfere with our comparison.

Preferred:
   young: Cune Rioja
   mature: Cune Gran Reserva

Alternatives:

young: Bodegas Bilbainas Rioja
Marqués de Murrieta Rioja

mature: Bodegas Bilbainas Reserva or Gran Reserva
Marqués de Murrieta Reserva or Gran Reserva

Vintages: Whatever is available where you can match the youthful and older wines of the same producer.

Consumerism. Rioja is an excellent value to anyone who enjoys very dry, woody and powerful Bordeaux-type wines. The older ones are still under-priced, and one wonders how long the supply can last. The few Northern Italian wines that trickle into this country are also an exceptional value, and their vintage dates probably,are a more accurate reflection of reality than the Spanish. Their style is more earthy and Burgundian, and because they haven't stayed in wood as long as the reservas they are more fruity and powerful. If you can find any older Chiantis to compare to young ones, do so. Even better than these are the well-aged wines from Lombardy and Tuscany. Look for some seven years old at least, to match with the nearest modern fare.

SOIL

This book was actually born from the struggles I had trying to understand an obscure phrase: *goût de terroir.* Literally, this means "the taste of the soil"—an unappetizing thing if taken literally. Obviously what it refers to is the much more subtle influence on the taste of the wine imparted by the terrain in which the grapes are grown. Graves, the major dry white wine area of Bordeaux, derives its name from its gravelly soil, and the Chablis and Champagne areas are known for their chalky substrata. You do not taste the rocks or the chalk, but a basic, specific dryness does come through which reminds you of those characteristics.

I was trying to explain this to a friend who was having difficulty separating that soil taste from the dryness imparted by the grape and the dryness of total sugar conversion. It is frustrating that you can't point a finger and say "there, that taste, that odd sensation of piquancy you're experiencing now, that is *goût de terroir.*" He wanted me to isolate that one taste so he could fix it in his mind and know where to look for it in all other wines. It is not a chemical taste that can be added to a wine; it is an influence that shapes taste.

The best way to illustrate *goût de terroir* is to use wines from the same grape variety grown in different places. Buy a Riesling from the Moselle, or the Rhine, one from California and one from, say, Chile. All are from the same grape and share the same basic grape taste. The essential difference is the soil (and climate) in which it is grown. The difference is, in part, the *goût de terroir*. Another easy way to taste *goût de terroir* is to buy a Beaujolais from the Haut-Beaujolais area. Beaujolais was originally divided into two classifications, Haut and Bas, specifically because of a distinct difference in soils. In the Haut area, the soil is granitic and contains a large amount of manganese, while in the Bas area it is chalky. Slate and gneiss produce wines with deep color and a bit of hardness in youth, such as Brouilly, Juliénas or Morgon. The softer, more delicate and easier-to-understand Beaujolais comes from vines grown on granite. The taste of the soil will therefore come through most clearly in something like a Morgon, so look for one from that group.

It is interesting that there are areas which have classified their wines according to the different tastes of the soil. As just illustrated, Beaujolais was one, but if you think about it, most regions base their classifications on the soil's effect.

The reason the Romanée-Conti vineyard makes a different wine from La Romanée's, though they are separated by only a footpath, is mainly because of the soil. Over the centuries vines may be replanted, cellar masters come and go, and weather over an entire region will average out the same. Yet, certain vineyards will constantly make finer wines than their neighbors. The reason must be the soil and exposure to the sun. Similarly, whose regions are broken up into Grand Cru, Premier Cru, and Commune Appellation vineyards primarily because of the quality of their soils.

Soil means a lot. You must consider its inherent taste and drainage characteristics. Drainage is important because the best wine is made where rain passes quickly through the earth and is not retained near the surface. That is why hilly areas with chalky or gravelly soil seem to work best. Well-drained soil is warmer and therefore the vine grows and ripens better. Drainage, of course, gives no taste of its own, but it does affect the final taste of the grape.

The chemical composition of the soil will influence the wine by dictating what minerals and nutrients are available for the vine to ingest. If the soil is acidic then the wine will be acidy. This can be good since acidity balances a wine; without acidity a wine would be flat and flabby. Soil composition in Santa Clara, south of San Francisco, is more acidy than that of the Napa Valley. A white wine such as Mirassou's extremely successful Gewürztraminer takes on added balance and complexity due to the more acidy soil. Comparing its taste to a Gewürztraminer put out by Louis Martini of the Napa Valley would be a worthwhile exercise.

TASTING 6: The Effects of Different Soil on the Taste of the Wine

	Region	*Producer*
Group I—Preferred:	California Riesling	Inglenook Riesling
	Moselle Riesling	Piesporter Gold-tropfchen Kabinett
	Rheingau Riesling	Rauenthaler Baiken Kabinett
	Chilean Riesling	Concha y Toro
Alternatives:	Any other wines of equal quality from the same regions.	

Group II—Preferred:	Chablis	Any from a reputable shipper
	Macon Chardonnay	La Forêt
	California Chardonnay	Inglenook Chardonnay
Alternatives:	Any other wines of equal quality from the same region. Any premier cru or grand cru Chablis. Any Macon Chardonnay. Any California Chardonnay but if it's available a Joseph Phelps, or Robert Mondavi, which are premium wines. Also see pages 174 and 175 for vintage information.	

Group III—Preferred:	California Pinot Noir	Inglenook Pinot Noir
	French Burgundy	Aloxe-Corton, Gevrey, Nuits-St-Georges
Alternatives:	Any California Pinot Noir of at least the same quality level. The Burgundy can be the same one used in tasting 2 on Pinot Noirs.	

Consumerism. Since the thing that is on trial here is the regions, use this tasting to explore which areas produce a wine in the style that you like. See if any price differential is warranted by an increase in quality or appeal.

WEATHER

The greatest vineyards and noblest grapes still suffer at the hands of the weather. Weather is the greatest variable in the making of a wine from year to year. The vines remain the same. The vinification methods don't change drastically, but year after year the wine differs, because of the wind, sun, rain, and temperature. Weather is not of major consequence to the vine in winter, but for the hundred days from the vine's full flowering in early June until the harvest in September or October, meteorological conditions are critical.

The first crucial influence comes when the vines flower. The more numerous the flowers, the more prolific the crop. The potential quantity of grapes is related to quality as well. If the vines bear very heavily, the nutrition from the ground must be spread over many clusters and the over-all vitality and quality is reduced. There must be a trade-off between the economic advantages of a large production and quality for a given year. What we are talking about is a correlation, not a direct proportion. An abundant harvest such as in Bordeaux in 1970 can produce top wines, but over-abundance will make quality suffer, as in the 1973 Bordeaux vintage.

During summer, growers hope for long, sunny days that are not too hot, with minimal amounts of rain. Most important of all is that the sun shine from mid-August, when the black grapes begin to gain color, until the harvest begins in late September or early October.

Weather can be a harsh mistress. Insufficient sun can leave the grapes unripe, lacking in sugar and high in acid. Hail storms can tear through the leaves, robbing the plant of vitality and the grapes of the ability to ripen. It can also knock the grapes from the vine, devastating the vineyard. Just days before the 1973 harvest a ten-minute hailstorm tore through the vineyards of Châteaux Haut Brion and La Mission, destroying half the crop.

Rain is perhaps the most common villain. Vines grow best in soil that retains little moisture. A rainstorm will feed the plant's roots. The berries will swell and their juice will quickly become watery. A wine's flavor is in the grape's essence, not its dilution. The wealthier châteaux can afford to combat bad weather with expensive technology. Because

A vine "bud" during dormancy.

The bud begins to swell in early spring.

With "bud break", the first leaf unfolds.

More leaves follow as bud "pushes" outward.

Shoot grows rapidly and floral cluster
(*center*) emerges.

The floral cluster before bloom looks
like tiny bunch of grapes.

The floral cluster in full bloom.

After flowering, blossoms "set" into miniature grape berries.

Adverse weather and/or incomplete pollination results in "shatter." Note some flowers have dried without setting, others set with incomplete pollination (shot berries). Large berries are normal mid-June size.

By early July berries have doubled in size several times.

Mature grapes awaiting harvest and transformation to wine.

of the baronial price of their wines, Mouton Rothschild can now afford to expose wet grapes quickly to artificially dry air prior to fermentation to evaporate any excess moisture on the outside of the skins. In spring, if frost is feared, Château Haut Brion sends a helicopter aloft to force warmer air down on the new buds. Haut Brion also takes infrared pictures to see if the fields are draining properly. Yet all the talent and all the will cannot make up for bad weather. In France it seems that three out of ten years are flops, six more vary from good to excellent, and maybe once in a decade is a real winner.

How the weather is distributed over the course of a summer also dictates quality. A growing season may have ten inches of rain and it can cover that 100-day period with continuous mist and showers and hence little sun, or else come early in the season with a few heavy but beneficial downpours. It is the same thing with temperature distribution. One year the sun may be constant and in the following, it might zoom the temperature up in the Spring and supply little warmth in the Fall and yet the number of degree days will be the same.

This type of weather variance affects the grapes. Overly damp air weakens the plant, making it susceptible to disease. Insufficient sun will retard a fruit's ripening. Too much sun will ripen the grapes too soon, producing a flat, alcoholic wine without compensating acidity. A good, balanced year is important.

Many stores carry or even promote some of the most well-known French vineyards from the off years of 1968, 1972 or 1974. To some people the label is the only key, so they buy these years and are disappointed. There are many advantages to these years, however, if you know what to expect. It is a way of trying some of the great names at a fraction of their normal price. The first growths are worth perhaps four or five dollars, but will probably be marked higher. They are made from the same vines and with the same extraordinary care that goes into a fine year, only the weather was against them. The wines have no staying power, will be rough and watery—but behind it all there will be the complexity and breeding of one of the world's great wines. Certain vineyards, in fact, have a small reputation for being able to produce a better wine than the poor year would seem to permit. Latour is one, Ducru-Beaucaillou another. There was a time when Lafite had too much pride to sell its wine under its own name in a bad year. Now the wine is simply too valuable to waste, and all years are bottled. Only the most successful barrels are bottled. Nevertheless I think they betray their quality image by doing this.

Trying an off year of a wine can tell us to what degree the weather influences the end product. If, as happened in Bordeaux in 1972 and 1968, there is much rain and little sun, the wines turn out thin, weak and watery, with a taste of damp cellars. The risks for the vineyard owner are enormous. In 1964, the crop appeared superb until harvest. The 1964 harvest started in some vineyards in Médoc the week of September 26. They were lucky. Those who waited to catch extra sun until the first of October were hit by three days of rain. The grapes swelled and some rotted. Three days without rain but also without sufficient heat could not dry out the grapes, and the rot spread. Then on October 6 the rain began again. Some owners carefully separated their ripe grapes from the bad ones. Some say Léoville Las-Cases was careful. Some say Lynch-Bages that year was not. Those châteaux of Médoc who harvested early were safe, but those who waited to get the extra few days of ripening lost the gamble. Their wines were still tolerable, but they had that extra amount of "legal water" (rain) and consequently were not as successful as some of their neighbors. Exactly who harvested when is too complex to memorize. Instead, it is better to be able to recognize the influence of weather so you can properly view the wine in a quality perspective.

For tasting purposes, 1972 or 1974 wine from Bordeaux is ideal. A 1968 is acceptable, but such light years as these have little staying power and overage quickly. Usually six years is their limit. If you are fortunate enough to find a Premier Cru (that is, Lafite, Latour, etc.) for a low price, buy it; otherwise get the best quality name château, such as Lynch-Bages, Ducru-Beaucaillou, Cos-d'Estournel or Palmer.

Even in areas renowned for their excellent weather, each year is different. It was once said that all California vintages were alike, but common sense is now beginning to prevail, and more and more people are admitting that not every California year is a vintage year. In fact, California may receive as much as fifteen percent above normal sunlight in some years, and while differences may not be extreme, certain vintage years are clearly superior, such as 1974, 1968 or, if you find any, 1964. California is also subject to calamities of weather. In 1970 an early spring frost lowered grape production by half. Fortunately, excellent weather during the rest of the summer, combined with the reduced crop, yielded a high-quality vintage. The following year, 1971, was disappointing and 1972 was a disaster in many places.

For better or worse, the world's attention to fine wine centers on

France and Germany, and so the meticulous charting of their vintage quality has become general knowledge. Since less attention is paid to Italy, Spain, California and Eastern Europe, the world is thus less intent on the character of their weather. Ask even a wine buff to list Spain's best years (1962, 1964, 1966 and 1970), or to name a poor one (1959) and he will probably be speechless. The same man could probably discuss every Burgundy vintage since the excellent 1928 crop. Weather varies the world over, and attention to vintage dates can mean the difference between a fine wine and a mediocre one.

TASTING 7: The Effects of Weather on the Taste of the Wine

		poor	*fair*	*good*
Group I—Preferred:	Château Ducru-Beaucaillou	68,72,74	73	70,71,75
Alternatives:	Château Léoville-Las-Cases	68,72,74	73	70,71,75
	Château Rausan-Ségla	68,72,74	73	70,71,75
	Château Lafite	68,72,74	73	70,71,75
	Château Latour	68,72,74	73	70,71,75
	Any Bordeaux Château			

		weak	*medium*	*strong*
Group II—Preferred:	Inglenook Cabernet Sauvignon	72	71	70,73,74
Alternatives:	Beaulieu	72	73	71
Group III—Preferred:	Chablis	72,74	70,73	69,71,75
Alternatives:	Any premier or grand cru			

Consumerism. I pay special attention to vintage when laying down wines. The fine names are so expensive now that it is worthwhile to buy only those from exceptional years. The difference in the price of one Bordeaux château in 1969 and 1970 may be twenty percent, but the 1970 is a vastly superior wine. We have been blessed recently with an unusual number of superior years. Get to know them. Don't ignore the others; try them too. But if you are buying in quantity, go for the best years. Of course, it's not as simple as it sounds. The vintage year is not the same everywhere in a country. Even within regions there are micro-climates. Some Pomerol châteaux believed they made better wines in 1967 than in the more highly-touted 1966. In Bordeaux, 1976 was a bit of a flop, while in Burgundy it was a blessing.

Be guided by what is written about a vintage, but learn to taste and evaluate for yourself.

TEMPERATURE

Temperature in the context of wine growing is a factor separate from weather. It may rain, hail, or shine at a wide variety of temperatures. A grape vine begins to grow in the spring, when daily temperatures probably average 50°F. What is important to the success of the vine is the total number of days on which the temperature is 50°F. or more. In 1930 two professors at the University of California at Davis noticed that by adding up the excess degrees for each day over 50°F. for the entire growing season (in California from April to October), the amount of excess warmth, called day-degrees that a specific vineyard area receives could be determined. They found that there are five basic temperature regions. The coolest is Region I, with 2,500 day-degrees or less, and the warmest is Region V, with over 4,000 day-degrees.

Grapes do not grow best in warm climates. Too much sun and heat ripen them too quickly, resulting in lower acidity which can't balance the sugar. The result is a flat, characterless wine. Algeria is the warmest of the major wine countries, with 5,200 degree-days, and its wines are in fact flabby and unimpressive. By contrast, Bordeaux rates 2,590 degree-days, Beaune (Burgundy) 2,519 and Geisenheim (German Rhine) only 1,709. The Napa and Sonoma Valleys fall into Regions I and II. Grapes grow best in a narrow band of temperature and climatic conditions.

California is a prime example of the effects of temperature on the character of wine. Gallo, Franzia, and other major commercial wine producers have vineyards located in the warm central valley of Southern California (Region IV). The premium producers are up north in the Napa and Sonoma areas. Each has found the temperature region that suits the wines it produces.

An interesting and instructive temperature tasting can be done with a Zinfandel wine from the northern and southern parts of the state. (See Tasting 8.) The Zinfandel grape produces one of America's most unusual and enjoyable wines. Its origin is obscure and the subject of lively debates. All we know is that as of now it is grown only in the United States. From the Southern California areas, drunk young, it is the American equivalent of a light, refreshing Beaujolais. Grown in the northern premium regions, it can be black, powerful and complex, and improve with age. Note especially the difference in color. Temperature will cause it to vary enormously. The Grenache grape, for example, when grown in cooler Northern California, is a full red. By the time you are in Davis (west of Sacramento) it is much lighter, and in Delano (north of Los Angeles) its juice is relatively clear with little color.

In summary: If your Zinfandel is thin and has a light color, then it probably came from a hot climate (or it may have been a rainy year in a cooler climate). If, on tasting, the wine is high in alcohol and low in acid, then it probably comes from a high-temperature region. If it tastes diluted, unbalanced and acidy, then poor weather is the cause.

This Zinfandel tasting is similar to the one done on page 62, except that here we isolate the effects of temperature. It is an elusive point to illustrate, because if we use jug wines from the hot Central Valley of California versus better quality wines from the cooler coastal regions, then the winemakers outfox us. A Zinfandel from the warm regions should turn out light, and it does, but then they blend into it a quantity of very dark grapes from another variety to reinforce the color. So we must scratch this test. The best example we can come up with would be two Zinfandels from the same reputable producer from two years, say 1972 versus 1974, and compare them. The chart on page 174 should be helpful.

Since the success of this tasting is subject to the capriciousness of availability of supply, we will use an abbreviated tasting format.

TASTING 8: Temperature

Preferred: Sebastiani Zinfandel 1972 and 1974

Alternatives: Inglenook Zinfandel 1972 and 1974
Any similar wine from reputable wineries

Consumerism. There is only mixed advice that can be given about temperature. Wines that are grown in hot climates usually are less interesting, though with care there can be exceptions. On the other hand, a hot year will often be a good one, so generally favor cooler regions in warm years.

COLOR

The color of a wine is the easiest clue to its quality, age, and origin. Our sense of sight is much more refined than our palate. Color has more than esthetic appeal. It is a statement of what the wine is and what has happened to it, the obvious product of weather, temperature, age, soil, and storage conditions.

The first thing to notice is the clarity of the wine. Haziness or cloudiness are bad signs. They may mean only that the sediment from the bottom of the bottle has been stirred up—unfortunate but not disastrous. That would cause a murkiness of taste, making the wine not as clean or refreshing as it should be. But cloudiness may also mean improper storage or vinification. A red table wine of three to five years of age should be bright in tint, with little sediment. An older wine would ordinarily be expected to have shown more of a deposit but still be clear.

The depth of color is a major clue to where the wine came from, and its "style." As the wine's color is thin, so too is the wine thin. This thinness may actually be delicacy, as in a rosé, and thus be desirable. On the other hand, if the color is not intense, you are dealing with a lighter style wine. If a wine from a known area and grape yields a lighter color than expected, something is amiss. It may come from a more southern and warmer climate. Higher temperatures can rob the wine of color. Cooler climates usually yield wines of greater body, more finesse, and deeper color. Thus, intensity of color is an important factor in prejudging a wine.

Such brash generalizations always get an author into trouble. Aside from the factors above, one thing that absolutely controls the color is the vintner. The longer he leaves the newly pressed wine on the skins (lees), the more color it picks up. Pigmentation is closely tied to tannin and more subtly to flavor. Thus, a deep full color is a good sign.

The *intensity* of color is simply the amount of red-purple present. It is like a measure of *density*. A totally different criterion is the *hue*—the amount a wine varies from a red-purple and toward an orange or tawny brown. This would tell the wine's health or age. The changes in color in a red wine are due to the precipitation out of solution of certain pigments. This condensation of sediment causes the yellow-brown color of tannins to become more noticeable. The slow, natural oxidation of the pigments also increases the brownness. Most of the red color remains, but an old wine moves toward a bricklike tint, similar to Indian red. I find that Burgundies take on this characteristic more quickly than Bordeaux. Except in extreme cases, it designates a nice, mature bottle of wine.

If the edges of the wine are orange and rather thin, and the wine is young, then the weather was probably poor. Without proper sun the grapes won't mature and darken. You can't make red wine from green grapes (unless you are unscrupulous and add ox blood). No year is so poor that there won't be any color, but it will be obvious that it won't have the dark purple robe of a hearty year.

The processes are similar, though without the initial red-purple robe, in white wines. A young Riesling should come out of the bottle as a sparkling light gold tinged with green. As it ages the color will become more noticeable (a full golden wheat) and later, if it is overaged, it will turn amber. Fresh, simple whites meant to be drunk young must have a little color. The great white Burgundies, Sauternes and Germans which need aging will show a healthy color.

TASTING 9: Color

One does not really hold a tasting for color. It is something one observes in a wine, something that should be studied consciously in each of the other tastings. One curious experiment you could do is to ask your local wine store for a bad bottle of wine. If the fellow doesn't choke, he might reach under the counter for one that someone has returned. Check its color; something will show.

V

QUALITY
RECOGNITION

It is much more important for a wine taster to be able to judge the quality of a wine than to be able to name its region or origin. To be able to identify the exact château and year from a sniff of the glass is a parlor game. It is pleasant if you can do it, but then it is more of a testimony to your memory than to your palate. Many famous men in wine are weak on identification. A wine taster is a judge, not a detective. A well-known writer, a director of Château Latour, asked when was the last time he mistook a Bordeaux for a Burgundy, replied "not since lunch."* But that same man can taste a raw young wine, fresh from the barrel, and tell you its future. Which knack is more valuable?

Cheap wine is obviously good or bad. It has no pretentions. If it is appealing, it is good; if it is not, it is bad. Only with fine wine is there the play of judgment. The majority of wine produced in the world is mass-manufactured to be a beverage to accompany meals and is meant to be drunk within the year. Even within the finest wine-growing regions, only a small fraction of the production is fine wine. This fine wine depends on aging for its complexity, and during this maturation it can pass through bad periods when it may not be pleasant to drink,

---

* Like "the king of wines, the wine of kings" etc., I have heard this remark claimed by many men and my stomach churns each time it is repeated to me as original.

VIN DE BORDEAUX

PRATS

1973

Médoc

Appellation Médoc contrôlée

CONTENTS 12,5 FL. OZS   ALCOHOL II % BY VOLUME
PRODUCED AND BOTTLED IN FRANCE

PRATS
PRATS FRÈRES
NÉGOCIANTS ÉLEVEURS, SAINT-ESTÈPHE (GIRONDE) FRANCE
PRODUCE OF FRANCE

These two labels are *not* the same. Médoc is a specific area within the Bordeaux region. The smaller area is always preferred to the larger classification. The key phrase is *Appellation Médoc/Bordeaux Contrôlée.*

VIN DE BORDEAUX

PRATS

1973

Bordeaux

Appellation Bordeaux contrôlée

WHITE BORDEAUX WINE

CONTENTS 12,5 FL. OZS   ALCOHOL II % BY VOLUME
PRODUCED AND BOTTLED IN FRANCE

PRATS
PRATS FRÈRES
NÉGOCIANTS ÉLEVEURS, SAINT-ESTÈPHE (GIRONDE) FRANCE
PRODUCE OF FRANCE

1973

33 Cantenac

Dear Cousin,

I'm delighted the 1971 was so well received. Herewith the 1973. You will find it similar in style but a little lighter and with more fruit. This is characteristic of the vintage. The summer weather of the two years was remarkably similar but the weather in June was better in 1973 than in 1971. This meant the flowering was more successful in 1973, the crop larger and the wine consequently lighter. I think you will find it an excellent wine, and I'll be interested to hear which you prefer.

Kindest regards, Yours Sincerely,
Peter A. Sichel

SHIPPED BY SICHEL & FILS FRÈRES, NÉGOCIANTS A BORDEAUX - GIRONDE

RED BORDEAUX WINE   **SICHEL**   PRODUCED AND BOTTLED IN FRANCE
Schieffelin & Co. — New York
IMPORTERS SINCE 1794   SOLE U.S. DISTRIBUTORS

LIQUID CONTENTS : 1 PINT 8 FLUID OZS   ALCOHOL 11,5 % BY VOL.

These two labels say essentially the same thing. They both contain a blend of grapes from all over the Bordeaux region. The key phrase is *Appellation Bordeaux Contrôlée.* The other important item is the shipper's name: Sichel and Prats. Both have excellent reputations.

RED BURGUNDY WINE
PRODUCT OF FRANCE

CONTENTS 1 Pt. 8 Fl. Oz.
ALCOHOL 12,5% BY VOLUME

Côte de Beaune-Villages

APPELLATION CONTROLÉE

MIS EN BOUTEILLES PAR

MOILLARD

NÉGOCIANT A NUITS-Sᵀ-GEORGES (COTE-D'OR)

Imported by AUSTIN NICHOLS & Cº Inc.

TABLE WINE   NEW-YORK, N. Y.

These two labels are *not* the same. The bottom one will be superior.
Côte de Beaune is the larger region within which the town of
Puligny is found. Montrachet is the most famous vineyard in the town
and is tagged onto the commune name for prestige.

Moillard is the negociant or shipper. We do not know
exactly who grew the grapes but Moillard takes responsibility
for making the wine and that is implied by "Mis en
bouteilles par Moillard" which also means it is not estate bottled.

WHITE BURGUNDY WINE
PRODUCT OF FRANCE

CONTENTS 1 Pt. 8 Fl. Oz.
ALCOHOL 12,5% BY VOLUME

Puligny-Montrachet

APPELLATION CONTROLÉE

MIS EN BOUTEILLES PAR

MOILLARD

NÉGOCIANT A NUITS-Sᵀ-GEORGES (COTE-D'OR)

Imported by AUSTIN NICHOLS & Cº Inc.

TABLE WINE   NEW-YORK, N. Y.

Table wine just
means wine as you
and I know it;
unfortified with
additional alcohol.

but not be a bad wine. It is necessary to learn to recognize the fine qualities that will develop behind this screen of "off" taste.

The quality of a wine and its character are determined by what it is made from, where it is made, how it is fermented and how it is matured. But what property must a wine contain in order to be a fine wine? Complexity. A cheap wine asks for or requires no more thought than a glass of milk. A fine wine on the other hand, commands your attention because of its complex and harmonious blending of subtle bouquets and tastes. A fine wine is obvious even to an inexperienced wine drinker. It has certain objective qualities that set it apart from the single-track taste encountered in a mass-manufactured wine. A novice may not appreciate these qualities, but he should recognize them.

Even a cheap wine, one without any outstanding character or defect, has some complexity. There is no one point at which you suddenly can say that now the wine is complicated enough to be called fine. Quality is a continuum; most wine occupies middle ground. Yet before you drink a wine there are hints that can help tell you how good it will be.

If you are well enough informed, a wine's reputation is, of course, the best thing. Unfortunately we usually have this intelligence available to us only on popular and famous wines. For the rest, our best source of information is the label.

There should be a rule written somewhere that *the more specific an area a wine comes from, the better it is likely to be* (in comparison with wines from the same region but from a larger area). In other words, if a bottle lists a specific vineyard as its origin, it will most likely be superior to one whose grapes are drawn entirely from throughout the surrounding region.

The name of a wine usually tells you its origin. A Bordeaux is from Bordeaux; a Hochheimer is from the German town of Hochheim; and a Burgundy should be from Burgundy. Alas, the reputations of certain wines are so prestigious in the public mind that other countries often copy the famous place names and put it on bottles of their own consistently inexpensive and inferior wines. A California Burgundy is not a Burgundy; it is an imposter whose origins are shrouded in innuendo and whose cure usually lies near an aspirin bottle. A Spanish Burgundy is worse. It properly infuriates a true Burgundian that so much insipid brew impersonates his own worthwhile wine, thus prostituting his art.

The triple curse of insincerity, callousness and greed brought on the Appellation Contrôlée (A.C.) laws. Their origins may be traced to the Champagne riots of 1911. Local growers pillaged a Champagne firm that had purchased inferior wines from outside the district and then blended and doctored them to create the characteristics of Champagne. In response to four months of insurrection, the government was forced to pass stringent measures controlling the marketing and production of Champagne, making it virtually impossible to pass off imitation Champagne as real. From this and similar measures evolved a set of laws known as Appellation Contrôlée, (A.C.) which is a geographic (location) and name control. In order to be worthy of bearing the label of a specific region or town, a wine had to be from that area and pass quite a few quality-control tests. If it failed the test, it could not use the name.

What unifies growers in all the important wine-producing regions of the world is their desire to produce the finest wines possible. In order to facilitate this, they seek to differentiate the best wines from the others. Since quality is most dependent on location, the grading structure for quality reflects where a wine originates: Region, commune or village. These ratings act as a guarantee to the consumer and, in turn, protect the producer from having his reputation spoiled by a neighboring competitor who puts out an inferior product.

BORDEAUX

The Haut-Médoc

Bordeaux produces one-half billion bottles per year of good, bad or indifferent wine. The trick is to find out which is which. The way to begin is with a geography lesson. Bordeaux is a region of Western

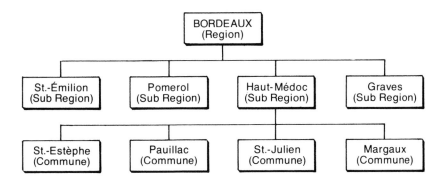

France through which the Gironde River flows. On the west bank of the river are the two famous wine-growing areas, the Haut-Médoc and Graves. On the opposite bank and to the east of the river are the smaller growing areas of St.-Emilion and Pomerol. All of these areas contain small townships or communes. The Haut-Médoc is divided into seventy communes, the most important of which are:

> Saint-Estèphe
> Pauillac
> Saint-Julien
> Margaux

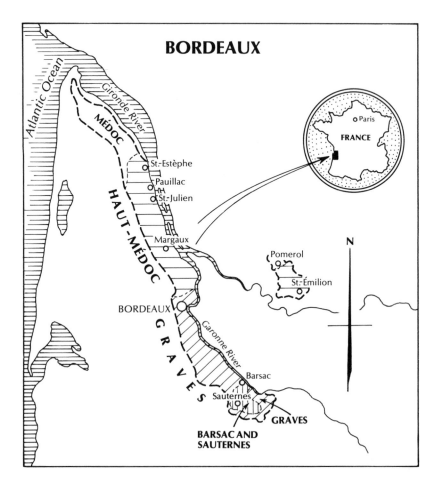

They are not far apart; from Saint-Estèphe to Pauillac is only four miles. But because of soil variation, micro-climates, etc., the wines have different characters. Even within the same town the wine will vary greatly. Together, these towns of the Haut-Médoc contain sixty châteaux which are generally regarded as producing the finest wine of the area. These estates were ranked into five categories, or "Cru," by a classification in 1855, that will be discussed later.

The red wines of Graves, St.-Emilion or Pomerol seldom mention a town of origin, so we needn't worry about subdivisions. There are other wine-producing areas within Bordeaux, such as Entre-Deux-Mers or Blayais, but their contribution to fine wine is minimal.

The finest wines produced in Bordeaux are all "château bottled." Château means an estate, and whether there is a regal palace or a shack on the property doesn't matter; it still is entitled to call its wine "château bottled" so long as the grapes come from that estate and have been bottled there. To be "château bottled" a label must say: "Mis

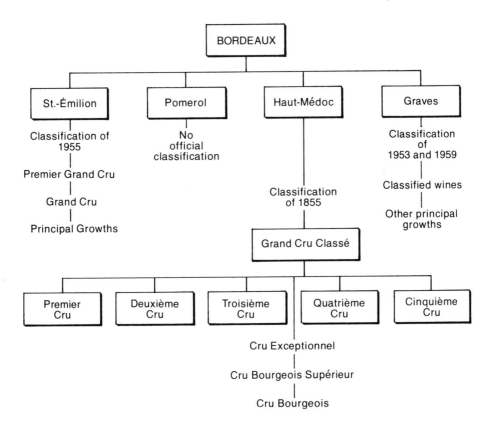

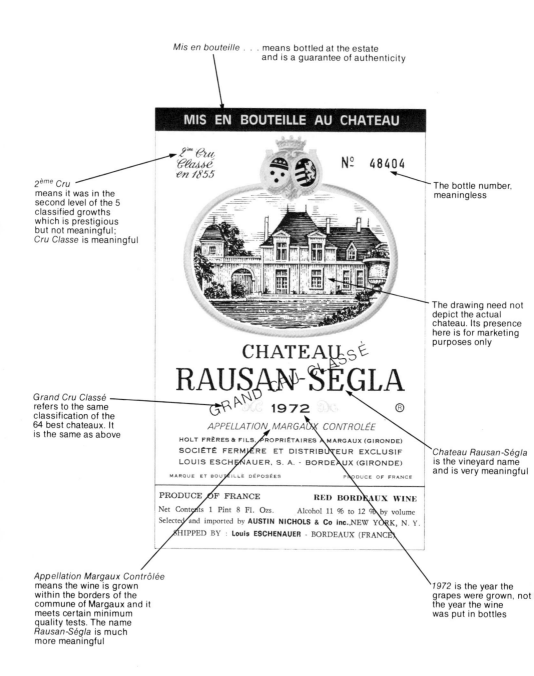

Mis en bouteille . . . means bottled at the estate and is a guarantee of authenticity

MIS EN BOUTEILLE AU CHATEAU

2ème Cru means it was in the second level of the 5 classified growths which is prestigious but not meaningful; *Cru Classe* is meaningful

2ᵉᵐᵉ Cru Classé en 1855

Nᵒ 48404

The bottle number, meaningless

The drawing need not depict the actual chateau. Its presence here is for marketing purposes only

CHATEAU RAUSAN-SÉGLA
GRAND CRU CLASSÉ
1972
APPELLATION MARGAUX CONTROLÉE

Grand Cru Classé refers to the same classification of the 64 best chateaux. It is the same as above

HOLT FRÈRES & FILS, PROPRIÉTAIRES A MARGAUX (GIRONDE)
SOCIÉTÉ FERMIÈRE ET DISTRIBUTEUR EXCLUSIF
LOUIS ESCHENAUER, S. A. - BORDEAUX (GIRONDE)
MARQUE ET BOUTEILLE DÉPOSÉES   PRODUCE OF FRANCE

PRODUCE OF FRANCE   RED BORDEAUX WINE
Net Contents 1 Pint 8 Fl. Ozs.   Alcohol 11 % to 12 % by volume
Selected and imported by **AUSTIN NICHOLS & Co inc.**,NEW YORK, N. Y.
SHIPPED BY : **Louis ESCHENAUER** · BORDEAUX (FRANCE)

Chateau Rausan-Ségla is the vineyard name and is very meaningful

Appellation Margaux Contrôlée means the wine is grown within the borders of the commune of Margaux and it meets certain minimum quality tests. The name *Rausan-Ségla* is much more meaningful

1972 is the year the grapes were grown, not the year the wine was put in bottles

en bouteille au Château" or "Mis en bouteille par le Propriétaire," which literally means put in the bottle at the Château or put in the bottle by the owner. Any other phrasing is meaningless. "Mis en bouteille par Bartin & Guestier," for example, means only that the firm of Barton & Guestier (B&G) bottled the wine. It doesn't say where it is from.

If a wine is not château-bottled it is unlikely it will be of top quality. A château-bottled wine will vary in quality according to the commune it comes from and the skill of the vintner. In 1855 a commission was set up to rate temporarily, in terms of quality, the major châteaux of the Haut-Médoc for an agricultural exhibit in Paris. Of course, there ensued terrible arguments, and the only method the commission could devise was to say that the best wines were those that had historically commanded the highest prices in the market place. They grouped the major châteaux into five "growths."

GRAND CRU CLASSE

Premier Cru*	1st Growth	4 + 1 Châteaux
Deuxième Cru	2nd Growth	15 Châteaux
Troisième Cru	3rd Growth	14 Châteaux
Quatrième Cru	4th Growth	10 Châteaux
Cinquième Cru	5th Growth	18 Châteaux

Only four châteaux were felt qualified for the top rank, "Premier Cru." They were: Châteaux Lafite, Latour, Margaux and Haut Brion. In 1973 the list was amended to include Mouton Rothschild. All five growths are collectively referred to as the Grand Crus. If a Châteaux belongs anywhere in this group you will most likely see "Grand Cru Classé" on its label. Since there obviously were more than 61 châteaux in Médoc, the hundreds of other estates which are collectively referred to as "petits châteaux" were also classified and were grouped as Cru Exceptionnel, Cru Bourgeois Supérieur or Cru Bourgeois, according to their quality.

In the last 120 years the quality of many of these wines has changed. There has been persistent pressure to revise the classification. In general, however, it remains accurate. Its main drawback is that people interpret it too rigidly. Each year any château may make a more suc-

---

* There was a time when I thought that premier cru was the first pressing of the grapes; deuxième cru the second, and cinquieme cru the very dregs. I was young and lived in Philadelphia and that may partially explain my ignorance.

cessful wine than its place in the rating would suggest. The reverse is also true. In addition, certain châteaux listed over a century ago as Cru Exceptionnel or Cru Supérieur, such as Château Chasse-Spleen or Château Phélan-Ségur, deserve to be included with the Grand Crus. It's the old lesson again; the label is only an indication, in order to know you must try.

Graves

Also sharing the westerly side of the river with the Médoc is the smaller area of Graves. The name Graves derives from its gravelly soil, which imparts a smoothness and a less assertive quality to its wines than one would find in its Haut-Médoc cousins. While the vast majority of wines from this area are white, there are some superlative reds. There are four leading communes in Graves, but because wines here are marketed under the regional Graves name, the townships are unimportant.

St-Emilion

Opposite the Haut-Médoc and inland from the river lies St-Emilion. It contains fifteen communes, but, again, none of their names is important. There was a classification here in 1955, one hundred years after the famous one in the Haut-Médoc. The top fourteen châteaux are listed as Premier Grand Cru (first great growths) and the next sixty-two are Grand Cru. Below these are estates called Principal Growth. The marketing men had learned their lesson. You will notice how much more tactful it is to class a wine "Principal Growth" than "Bourgeois Supérieur."

Pomerol

Pomerol borders St-Emilion but is much smaller. There has been no official ranking, as the estates are small and frequently change hands. Consequently there will be no official phrase on the label other than "Appellation Pomerol Contrôlée." Unofficially, Château Petrus is recognized as the outstanding growth of the area, followed by eighteen other Superior Châteaux.

In summary, there are two methods of classification applicable to Bordeaux: First you distinguish by region; then, within the region, there is usually a ranking of comparative merits.

The simplest rule to follow is that wine must be grown within a region to be able to label itself as originating there. If a wine is labeled Bordeaux Supérieur, then the grapes must have been grown in the Bordeaux region, though they may come from different areas of Bordeaux. Some may come from Talais in the north and some from La Réole nearly one hundred miles to the south. But not all wine from all areas of the district is the same. Some towns produce better wines than others.

In Bordeaux such a town would be Pauillac. Within its boundaries are such luminaries as Châteaux Lafite Rothschild, Mouton Rothschild, Latour, Pichon-Longueville and a host of other world-famous châteaux. What is implied is that with so much fine wine being produced in this one small area, any wine from Pauillac, even if it is an unknown label, should be of superior quality. Needless to say, Pauillac doesn't want just any grower using the name of its town, even if he does meet the qualifications set by the regional A.C. laws. So they have set up laws even more stringent than those applied to the region. The first rule is obvious: The grapes must have been grown exclusively within the borders of the commune. In addition, the grapes must be capable of producing a good wine on their own: no sugar is allowed to be added (chaptalization) to the unfermented pressed grapes to increase the wine's natural alcoholic content. Thus if a Bordeaux wine has a twelve percent alcohol level stated on its label, it should have come there through the hard work of nature, not the intervention of man. That healthy level implies that the weather was good, that the grapes matured, and that, consequently, there was plenty of natural sugar produced to convert into alcohol.

The ultimate in restricting the use of the name is when you are dealing with the most specific piece of land, the individual château itself. The wine must come from the land classified as belonging to that château in 1855 or be of an equivalent classification. At the château level, many are trying to make the finest wines possible. The vicissitudes of the châteaux are constantly watched, and any quality loss is an immediate source of rumor.

What all this means to us is that the more specific the area a wine comes from, the better it is likely to be. A wine labeled simply A.C. Bordeaux Supérieur can come from anywhere in Bordeaux and should not be as good as one labeled Haut-Médoc. A commune wine such as Pauillac, St. Julien, Margaux, etc, would be better still, and the top of the range is the château. And so it goes from general to specific, from a drinkable beverage to a work of art.

TASTING 10: Bordeaux Overview

Preferred— 1. Regional: Mouton Cadet
one of each: 2. Communal: Sichel's St. Julien
3. Estate-bottled: Château Ducru-Beaucaillou

Alternatives: 1. Any Bordeaux Supérieur (A.C.) preferably from Sichel or Ginestet
2. Any commune wine (e.g., A.C.-Pauillac or St.-Émilion) preferably from the same shipper as above
3. Any of the top classification (grand or premier cru classé) estate-bottled wines preferably from the same commune and year as your selection #2.

Consumerism. You may notice something very odd: You may prefer the communal wine over the château wine. Considering the inflation in prices, it is hardly likely that you will be buying an older vintage. The communal wine, being simpler, might well be showing better, but hopefully under the austere strength of the château wine you should be able to detect the promise of a future development which the commune wine doesn't offer. If you are buying for present consumption stick with the commune, but also get a few bottles of the other and lay them away.

It is quite possible that you may find the taste of the château wine to be undecipherable when it is young. Try this simple trick: Let it sit in a glass and retest it every few hours or overnight. If you do the same with the commune wine, you should see the one develop and the other fade.

BURGUNDY

The study of each wine area requires a different approach. The easiest is probably Bordeaux, because it is already so highly organized by the classification of 1855. Burgundy is something else again. It is more than just one region. We may think of it as that small area, centered in Beaune, that produces many of the world's most famous red wines, plus a tiny yield of white. Actually, within its historic borders lie Chablis, the Mâconnais and Beaujolais as well as the Côte d'Or, the area we usually think of as Burgundy. In Bordeaux the vineyards are inherited or sold intact. In Burgundy, perhaps because it is older and had its roots in another age, inheritance laws have subdivided

vineyards to such an extent as to make the nature of the wine from any
one vineyard quite unpredictable. Some vineyards are so divided that
they may be owned and harvested by as many as sixty individuals. One
owner may even have some nonadjacent sections of the same vineyard.
It is also likely that he would own small pieces of other vineyards as
well.

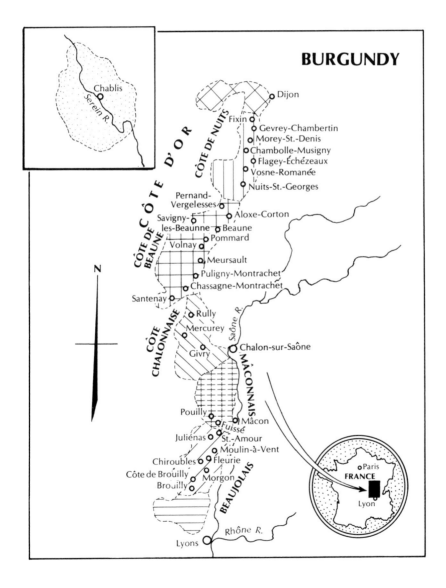

Thus, in Burgundy the man who produces the wine is perhaps more important than where the wine comes from. To help organize the confusion, Burgundy has developed a four-tier system of classification.

At the top are the thirty Grand Cru vineyards whose names are so famous and whose wines are so much in demand that they need put only their own name on a bottle in order to be recognized. Probably the most famous is Romanée-Conti, a vineyard of only four-and-one-half acres, which shows how rare these wines really are. Chambertin is only thirty-two-and-one-half acres. Even the largest, Clos de Vougeot, is only 140 acres, twenty percent smaller than Château Mouton Rothschild, which is, after all, only an average-size château.

Below these nobles stand the Premier Cru wines. These tie the name of their vineyard to the name of the commune. In Beaune, which has no Grand Crus, this would be *Beaune* Vigne de L'Enfant Jésus or *Beaune* Clos des Feves; in Vosne-Romanée, *Vosne-Romanée* Les Suchots. The fact that a wine is "only" a Premier Cru does not detract from its quality. In any one year a Premier Cru vineyard may make a more successful wine than a Grand Cru neighbor. The land gives you only the *potential* for making a great wine. It is the skill of the cellarmaster that is the telling factor. Thus, given a choice between a Premier Cru wine produced and bottled by Louis Latour, Louis Jadot, Joseph Drouhin or Bouchard, and a Grand Cru wine from a less exalted name, I would put my faith in the Premier Cru.

The reputation of the man or firm who produced the wine becomes even more important as you move to wider classifications. The third level will ordinarily bear only the commune or town name. This is a guarantee that the grapes were grown·within the boundaries of that

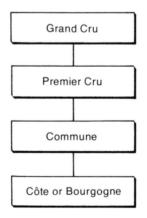

commune and not trucked in from less-qualified areas. This class is called "Appellation Communal." A wine will just label itself Beaune, Nuits-St-Georges or Gevrey-Chambertin. Occasionally, in smaller letters under the commune name, the producer may list the vineyard. It is his way of saying that that vineyard is worthy of special notice and stands above the average commune wine.

Not all Burgundy is great wine. The lowest level of the pyramid is simply called "Bourgogne" (Burgundy). Since the great wines are grown almost exclusively on the hills, these wines would come mainly from the plains to the south of the towns. They are common, occasionally good drinking wines, but without any complexity or breed. So the rule still is: The more specific the name, generally the better the wine.

The Appellation Contrôlée method of ranking is more than a guarantee of area of origin. It also means that the wines have been produced in accordance with certain objective standards. If the wine is red it must come from the Pinot Noir grape; if white, it comes from Chardonnay. The yield of grapes per acre is limited in order to guard against over-production and consequent loss in quality. Similarly, a minimum percentage of alcohol is required, higher in the finer wines than in the more common. If a wine is to qualify under the Appellation Contrôlée Laws for a given Appellation, it must meet legally-defined qualifications in pruning, viticulture, fertilization, vinification methods and aging as well.

The existence of so many owners of pieces of the same vineyard has led to consumer confusion. Coupling that confusion with the fact that vinifying just a few vines is economically unsound, a method had to be found that would simplify matters for grower and consumer alike. What has evolved is a system wherein a shipper (*négociant*) buys the wine of several owners of one vineyard, then combines them and markets them under his own name. He will blend for a consistency of style and taste from year to year. Such a man earns a reputation according to the quality of wines he buys, his skill in blending and his honesty in labeling. He knows that a century of honesty can be wiped out in a customer's mind by a single bad bottle.

There are several good Burgundies that are not great Burgundies. Many of these come from two of the other major wine-producing areas which still lie within the boundaries of Burgundy: The Mâconnais and Beaujolais. The Mâconnais starts twenty-five miles south of the Côte d'Or and Beaujolais perhaps thirty miles farther. Together they produce more wine than all the Côte d'Or, most of it red wine from the prolific Gamay grape. In recent years the enthusiasm for Beaujolais, especially in the United States, has far outrun any merit the wine might possess. Once it became a fad, an incredible amount of junk poured onto the market. Many such wines were thin, acidic, bitter and full of chemicals to stabilize the wine during its rough journey across the ocean. Even then many didn't survive. Some importers started charging $4.00 to $6.00 for a wine that is a pleasant *vin ordinaire*—outrageous! Without being chauvinistic, California was turning out better "Beaujolais" than the French stuff we New Yorkers were drinking from 1971–74.

With an introduction like that you may well question why I want you to start by tasting Beaujolais. First of all, there is a sound basis for its reputation. Beaujolais should be known as clear and unadulterated wine. From a reputable bottler they should be supple, fresh and fruity without any green harshness on the palate—a baby Burgundy. For the most part they are bottled young (within six months of harvest and with little to no cask aging) and should be drunk within the year. A few are more refined and can keep for several years. These latter are named for the various communes such as Fleurie, Morgon, Juliénas Chénas, Brouilly, and Moulin-à-Vent.

Beaujolais wine is a stepping-stone into the realm of Burgundy wines. It shows most of the charm without the aristocratic, heavier trappings of the bigger wines of Burgundy. There is a cousin-like relationship in taste and style.

TASTING 11: Burgundy Overview

Preferred	1. Beaujolais Jadot
(try one of each):	2. Brouilly
	3. Gevrey-Chambertin
Alternatives:	1. Any reputable shipper of Beaujolais-Villages
	2. Any heavier Beaujolais-Villages of the same year
	3. Any commune Burgundy but preferably coming from the northern sections such as Fixin, or Morey-Saint-Denis.

Consumerism. Burgundies, as we will demonstrate later, are currently made lighter and fruitier than they once were. If you prefer a heavier, more old-fashioned wine, something closer to a traditional Burgundy, then experiment with bottles from the Côte Rôtie and the Côtes-du-Rhône. These regions are almost due south of Burgundy and still produce enormous, full-bodied wines for very acceptable prices. For contrast, you may enjoy including one of them in the Burgundy overview tasting.

GERMANY

"Everything as before. There is no Rhine wine, so it's French wine. When they have no more virgins, then one must dance with the whores."—written by Frederick the Great of Prussia, a German wine lover and no friend of the French, in the margin of a letter to a field commander at the beginning of the Seven Years' War.

To my surprise, I frequently find many of my friends inhibited the first time they try a fine German wine. As beginners they cling to the outmoded generalization that the drier a wine, the better it is. They are unprepared for the generosity and rich ripeness that are the hall-marks of great Rhine and Moselle wines. My friends' doubts seldom last long, however, because these are some of the easiest wines to fall in love with. The light ones (light in taste and low in alcohol) are the most refreshing wines this side of a rosé. The heavier, sweet ones are the height of the winemakers craft. They are complex symphonies of taste, very rare and very expensive.

The reason German wines are so easy to understand is that they depend so noticeably on two criteria: bouquet and breed. The *bouquet* must always be clearly discernible and, in the best of cases, enormous. It will be composed of fruit and flower smells. It must be agreeable whether the wine is common or exceptional. The scent should be of a very ripe peach, plum or apple, but not those specific fruits. It should really be similar to them but differ in a way that intrigues. It should be complex in such a way that the tenth sniff should provoke associations different from the first.

The *breed* is the quality of the wine; how clear the tastes are, how complex and varied. Breed associates itself with taste and aftertaste, a clean, lingering finish. It is the sign of pedigree, the correct marriage of mature vines to the perfect site.

In these vineyards, which are at the northern limit of the world's wine growing zone, the grape lives within the narrowest limits of sur-

vival—and that is what makes German wines great. Virtually all the
best vineyards are planted exclusively in the Riesling grape. It has
been in the last 300 years that the superiority of this grape in this
place has been recognized. Compared to other grapes it produces little
wine, but the supreme sites use nothing else. If a bottle of wine is a
good wine, or bears a town name instead of a brand name such as
Liebfraumilch, and if no other grape is listed on its label, it is safe
to assume it is a Riesling. This is especially the case if the wine comes
from the two greatest regions: the Rheingau or the Moselle. If the
bottle is from one of the secondary regions, it may quite likely be

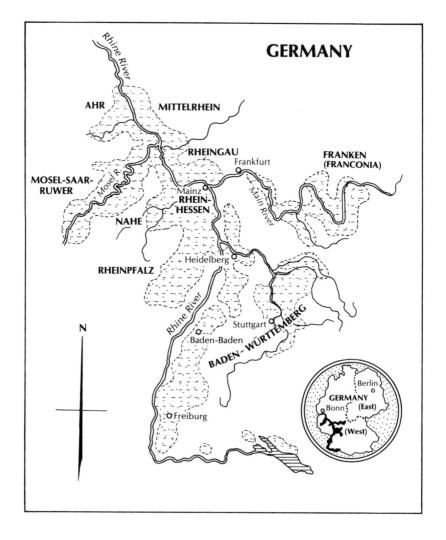

from one of two other grape varieties: The Sylvaner and the Muller-Thurgau. Both yield more juice per vine than the Riesling and so are favored where quantity is important. In a good year either grape will make a good wine, but it is only under the rarest of circumstances that someone will try to make something great from them.

German practices vary most noticeably from all others in that they alone produce many different qualities of wine from the same vineyard. In France or Italy all the grapes of a single variety are harvested at the same time and bottled together. In Germany, at the prestige sites, pickers will go out five or six times to gather progressively riper grapes. Each batch is vinified separately and is classed and labeled according to its ripeness. Although the new laws no longer permit this, as recently as the 1960s the producer could divide each of his six pickings into good, fine and finest batches. A single vineyard could thus produce eighteen or more wines. If each vineyard did this, the possible combination of labels would be greater than the number of angels that could fit on the head of a pin. The result was confusion to the consumer —and that's bad for business.

In 1971 the German Government attempted to deal with this superabundance of titles by reorganizing its wine laws. Its primary intent was simplification, consumer guidance and protection. First it said that all German wine falls into one of three quality categories which must be listed on the label:

qualitätswein mit prädikat

↑

qualitätswein

↑

tafelwein

The *tafelwein* is the *vin ordinaire* of Germany. They are light, uncomplicated table wines originating in one of five large growing regions. They are good daily drinking wines, but lack particular distinction. Most of them are consumed locally, as of now very little has reached our shores.

Qualitätswein is a superior quality of wine which originates in one of eleven specific growing regions. It is felt to possess more typical regional flavors than a *tafelwein*. *Qualitätsweins* are more than casual wines. Their taste will be more distinctive and individual.

The finest wines that Germany produces are the *qualitätswein mit prädikat* (Q.M.P.), or quality wines with special attributes. This is

PRODUCT OF
GERMANY

SICHEL

1974

Moselbluemchen

MOSELLE WINE

DEUTSCHER TAFELWEIN MOSEL

BOTTLED & SHIPPED BY

H. Sichel Söhne, Mainz

SCHIEFFELIN & CO. — NEW YORK

CONTENTS:
1 PINT 7 FL. OZS.

IMPORTERS SINCE 1794 · SOLE U.S. DISTRIBUTORS

German White Wine
Product of Germany

Alcohol 9% – 10% by Vol.
Contents: 1 Pint 8 Fl. Oz.

Mosel-Saar-Ruwer

1975

Piesporter Michelsberg

Qualitätswein

ST. URSULA WEINGUT UND WEINKELLEREI GMBH · BINGEN

SOLE U. S. AGENT

C & B Crosse & Blackwell Vintage Cellars SAN FRANCISCO, CA

A.-P.-Nr. 5 342 352 000 76

1975

Deidesheimer Rathaus 1532

AUS DEM LESEGUT DES
WINZERVEREINS NIEDERKIRCHEN/DEIDESHEIM

GERMAN WHITE WINE
PRODUCT OF GERMANY

ALCOHOL 8% – 9% BY VOL.
CONTENTS: 1 PINT 8 FL. OZ.

Deidesheimer Hofstück

RHEINPFALZ   Kabinett   A. P. Nr. 5 342 352 000 77

Qualitätswein mit Prädikat

SOLE U. S. AGENT   C&B Crosse & Blackwell Vintage Cellars   SAN FRANCISCO, CA.

ST. URSULA

WEINKELLEREI · BINGEN AM RHEIN

where wine becomes an art form. The vintner does not just suddenly cry "eureka" and declare a wine Q.M.P. The wine must be tested by the German government and pass stringent requirements. A wine must pass the minimum standards for alcoholic content (nine percent), be from approved regions and grape varieties, and also be graded on a point scale system for appropriate color, character, bouquet, taste, etc. Unless the wine amasses enough points collectively, it will not be given the right to call itself Q.M.P. If it fails, its rank will be reduced to *qualitätswein*, still a good wine but not quite as fine. What all this amounts to is a government guarantee of quality.

There are eleven wine regions in Germany; each of these, in turn, is divided into three or more subregions called *bereich*. The *bereich* comes into existence because there are some common taste factors that unify it. A wine that comes from grapes produced in the subregion might be labeled Bereich Bernkastel Riesling. If instead of the subregion it came from a specific town, it would be a *grosslage* or collection of vineyards labeled Bernkastl*er*—the final "er" in German means "from the town of." The final category is *einzellagen*, or individual vineyard, and this would have the specific name of the plot. As with all wine areas, the more specific an area a wine is from, the better it is likely to be.

All of this appears complicated because it is. But what existed before was worse. Previously there had been 30,000 vineyards entitled to their own names. Now by combining most vineyards of under twenty acres into groups, or *grosslage*, there are a scant 3,000 to remember. *Qualitätswein* refers to the quality; *bereich*, etc., refers to its origin.

> Region (Eleven)
> Bereich (Sub-Region)
> Grosslage (Group of Vineyards)
> Einzellagen (Individual Vineyard)

By now you may be a little bit puzzled as to where wines like Liebfraumilch, Moselblümchen or Zeller Schwartz Katz fit in. These popular wines are blends which don't come from one town but are from a limited growing area. They too must be labeled according to their quality, and the ones you will most likely see will be *Qualitätswein*. This is the minimum guarantee. Within this class there is a vast range in quality. It is up to you to find the shipper who makes the wine that suits you best.

Kellerei Hasensprung is the bottler/shipper

Rheingau is the general
wine growing region

J. Bäumer is the owner

Hattenheim is the village

Schützenhaus is the vineyard

Spätburgunder is the unusual grape

Spätlese means late picked, ripe grapes

Qualitätswein mit Prädikat is the
highest quality designation given
by the German government

A.P. Nr.—is the government
testing number

The greatest art of the German vintner lies in his ability to let the grapes on his vines mature to the maximum sweetness the weather will allow. It becomes progressively more of a gamble to leave grapes unharvested through October, November, December and even occasionally into January. The reward is that at first the grapes gain more sugar and will have more taste from natural ripeness. After a certain point the grapes can no longer ripen. What must occur next may be considered a fortuitous calamity: The grapes are attacked by a virus mold, *Botrytis Cinerea*, which makes the skins permeable. The water in the grapes evaporates and the grape shrivels like a raisin. The grapes become visually repulsive, but the main effect is that without the water the grapes are left with a concentrated essence of taste and bouquet. The process is enormously risky and time consuming, but the result can be spectacular. In recognition of this procedure of producing wines, the Government has divided up the Q.M.P. into five categories, according to the maturity and sugar content of the grapes:

Kabinett: A high quality, fully ripened wine usually harvested in October. The name originally meant a special quality wine reserved for the cabinet (wine cellar) of the producer or of a noble.

Spätlese: These are wines from late-picked grapes, which give the wine an added lushness.

Auslese: From the later picked grapes, which have been sorted and pressed separately from the rest.

Beerenauslese (BA): Wines from the ripe and overripe berries which include *some* raisin-like grapes attacked by the Botrytis (*Edelfäule* in German) mold. These rare and expensive wines possess an intense, flowery aroma and amber color.

Trockenbeerenauslese (TBA): This is the rarest of all German wines and is made exclusively from the shriveled Botrytised grapes. It may take a vintner two full days to find enough grapes to make one bottle. Nor is that the end of the difficulties. It is very difficult to ferment a wine that is as rich in sugar as this. It may take four times as long as a regular wine, but the end product should be a nectar capable of lasting and improving for decades.

Eiswein: An odd thing may happen to a ripe grape if there is a sudden frost: The water content will freeze. If those grapes are picked and lightly pressed before they thaw, the resulting wine will be rich in sugar and aroma. It would be quite similar to an Auslese, Beerenauslese, or even a Trockenbeerenauslese.

To receive a fair impression of the variety of German wines, one

RHEINGAU

Schloss Schönborn

1972er

Geisenheimer Schloßgarten
Riesling Kabinett

A. P. Nr. 31.052.012.73
Domänenrat
Erzeugerabfüllung der Gräflich von Schönborn'schen Kellerei Hattenheim
QUALITÄTSWEIN MIT PRÄDIKAT

Georg u. Karl Ludwig Schmitt'sches Weingut
Weingut Georgshof — Weingroßkellereien — Nierstein am Rhein

Weinbau   Weingüter in Nierstein, Oppenheim, Schwabsburg u. Dienheim   seit 1618

1937er

Niersteiner Grosser Auflangen
Terrasse-Riesling-Auslese-naturrein

Rheinhessen
Naturgewächs und Originalabfüllung

Weingut Villa Sachsen
ST. URSULA WEINGUT UND WEINKELLEREI · GMBH. BINGEN · RH.

German White Wine   ~ **ERZEUGERABFÜLLUNG** ~   Alc. 9%-10% by Vol.
Product of Germany   Contents: 1 Pint 8 Fl. Oz.

Binger Scharlachberg
RIESLING
SPÄTLESE
QUALITÄTSWEIN MIT PRÄDIKAT
Sole U. S. Agent C&B Crosse & Blackwell Vintage Cellars
RHEINHESSEN   SAN FRANCIS

RHEINGAU

Schloss Schönborn

1971er

Erbacher Marcobrunn
Riesling
BEERENAUSLESE

Domänenrat
A. P. Nr. 31.052.012.72
Erzeugerabfüllung der Gräflich von Schönborn'schen Kellerei Hattenheim
QUALITÄTSWEIN MIT PRÄDIKAT

Winzerverein Deidesheim
E·G·M·B·H

DEIDESHEIM

ÄLTESTE WINZERGENOSSENSCHAFT   DER RHEINPFALZ·GEGRÜNDET 1898

Deidesheimer Leinhöhle
Riesling Trockenbeerenauslese
Qualitätswein mit Prädikat   Erzeugerabfüllung
A. P. Nr. 5 106 320 21 72

RHEINPFALZ

should sample at least three. Since Liebfraumilch or one of the other regional blends is an inevitable example of reputable mass wines, it should be included.

TASTING 12: A German Overview

Preferred 1. Deinhard Green Label
(try one of each): 2. Deinhard Bernkasteler Lilac Seal
3. Wehlener Sonnenuhr

Alternatives: 1. Any wine drawn from an entire region:
a. Blue Nun
b. Zeller Schwartz Katz
c. Liebfraumilch
d. Moselblümchen

2. Any one bearing the name of a specific town but not yet a specific vineyard:
a. Bernkasteler Bereich
b. Niersteiner Bereich, etc.

3. Any estate-bottled wine labeled "Q.M.P." kabinett

Consumerism. A noteworthy phenomenon in German wines is highlighted by this tasting: Many of the finer, estate-bottled wines are actually less expensive than such heavily-promoted cousins as Blue Nun or good-quality Liebfraumilches, etc. Now, Blue Nun has its advantages. People who don't know wine can count on it. However, you know wine and you will find that exploring the "Q.M.P." wines will be infinitely more interesting and not more expensive.

ITALY

It has always been easy to identify an Italian wine: The names all end with a vowel. Until recently our perception of them has been almost that simplistic. We have been dominated by two or three well-recognized types. Everyone knows Chianti and Soave. A few may venture to try Verdicchio, Valpolicella—or wherever the restaurant's wine list may lead them for under six dollars. They are good wines to drink, and, if they aren't distinguished, well, who would notice alongside the tomato sauce? It is little wonder that they gained the reputation of being wines of enthusiasm and little more. But that characterization is both unfair and inaccurate. The Chianti Classico Riservas, for example, are wonderful wines, great values and easy to come by. The special care that has been taken in making and aging them has produced a superior wine. There are others as well that belie the myth of pedestrianism, wines such as Barolo, Spanna, Gattinara, and that most intriguing of all Italian red wines, the Brunello de Montalcino, which is supposed to live for more than a century. Part of the credit for the improvement belongs to the producers who dreamed high dreams; part belongs to the consumers who are prepared to seek out and appreciate such fine wines.

The origins of Italy's problems lie in its long peasant wine-growing tradition. It is a farming country that may well have been given too fine a gift as far as wine is concerned. Its climate is extremely favorable for the production of high-yield common grapes. Everywhere it produced considerable quantities of common wine, which made each region self-sufficient. Without internal or export trade there was little motivation for improvement. Italy became known for the quantity, not the quality, of its wines. Each farmer had his own crop, and that which he had to spare was sold to his cousin or friends, whose loyalty made allowance for taste. Each region and even each farmer had his own favorite blend of grapes, so that even today there are still one hundred different varieties in use.

Labeling became complicated. The farmer, because he was selling the product of his own hands, could call his wine whatever he wanted. Such a policy would not confuse his friends, who already knew the wine, and no one else was involved. What grew from this was a confusion which has yet to be resolved.

Even now an Italian label may mean different things. It may tell you the grape, or it may tell you the area from which it came, or it may just give you some fanciful title that appealed to the producer. This is a tribute to the extremely individualistic nature of Italians and to a country that still manages to produce a dizzying variety of wines—with an appealing inconsistency of skill.

Although it started belatedly, the Italian Government has recently been trying to take some of the confusion out of their wines. Strong quality-control laws have been passed—and are enforced. Export regulations have been set up. The wines reaching our shores are more consistent and are better made than they've ever been before. Those producers who want to make money in wine no longer plant their vines in cornfields or train them up olive trees. They've modernized. They use the most advanced techniques and equipment, and where they don't own all the land themselves, they require high standards for the grapes they buy. The major names such as Bolla, Ruffino or Ricasoli have too much to lose to be tempted to drop their standards. It is with the smaller people that there is both risk and reward.

Over the years the smaller producers have banded together into cooperatives to be able to afford modern equipment and technology, to market their product more easily and to command a better price. Later these and other associations in a region set up *consorzi*, or governing bodies, dedicated to the maintenance of standards in wine making, and the protection of their region's name. The first such group was, appropriately enough, from Chianti. It identified its special product by issuing a label for the neck of the bottle; only producers whose wine came from the right region and which met certain quality standards were allowed to use it. In this way the winemakers guarded Chianti's reputation and their own financial well-being.

This was thus the beginning of the Italian equivalent of the French Appellation Contrôlée laws. As an official policy the quality-control laws came into being in 1963, after some spectacular scandals involving the production and sale of "fabricated" wine concocted from previously-crushed grapes, skins, chemicals and ox blood (for color). The new laws govern the labeling, origin and quality of wines, and are intended to upgrade the quality and image of Italian wines abroad. The laws are national but do not cover all regions, which means that some perfectly good or perhaps excellent wine can appear without any of the classifications listed below. They will still have an INE seal, which is an export guarantee of quality.

INE means that the wine has been sampled by a government testing panel and has passed tests for minimum quality and trueness of character. There are three grades under this seal:

Denominazione Di Origine Controllata e Garantita (D.O.C.G.)
Denominazione Di Origine Controllata (D.O.C.)
Denominazione Di Origine Semplice (D.O.S.)

The D.O.S. is the simplest grade, and it is rarely exported. The D.O.C.G. is the top grade—and it hasn't been instituted yet; we probably won't start seeing it until 1981. In the meantime, the wines that meet this highest classification are still clustered with the D.O.C. So all we will encounter will be wines that are D.O.C., or else those not yet classified.

The D.O.C. is the "controlled" grade. It must come from the area listed on the label, achieve specific quality standards, and be produced in the traditional manner. Such standards and rules are usually proposed by the local consorzi.

Another phrase that may show up on the label is "classico," which means that the grapes come from the central area in which the wine was traditionally made, and not just from the permitted surrounding areas. The distinction may or may not be meaningful, depending upon the region and the specific producer involved.

The overabundance of Italian wines makes them confusing even to the professional. No one seems to have much perspective on the field, which is probably why all books on the subject are just disguised lists. They merely match geographic place names to the wines of the region, ignoring any attempt to relate the wines of one area to another. Yet, treated as a whole, there are distinguishably different styles within all Italian reds and whites.

TASTING 13: Italian Reds—A United View

Italian reds organize themselves more easily than do the whites. For the most part you can class the reds by "weight," running from refreshing, light wines such as Bardolino up to some of the world's weightiest, most emphatic wines like Brunello or Amarones.

It would be tedious and unrewarding work, as much for you as for me, to list the attributes of each of the major red wines, where they were made, how long they aged, etc. Instead, let's approach it as a continuum and see how much can be learned with relatively little effort. You can plump up our approach on your own if you want to concentrate on any one area. We do that by focussing on Chianti— in a later testing.

First break the reds up into light wines, medium, heavyweights and finally, the whoppers. Exclude Lambrusco; it may be a nice, fizzy form of grape juice containing alcohol but it's too close to "pop" wines to be taken seriously. The first of the wines to try is Bardolino. Think of Bardolino as a red you would drink during the summer, and its neigh-

RUFFINO

RISERVA DUCALE
Chianti Classico
DENOMINAZIONE D'ORIGINE CONTROLLATA

NET CONTENTS 1 PINT 8 FL OZ

ALCOHOL BY VOL. 13%

Wine produced and bottled in Italy by I. L. RUFFINO
IN PONTASSIEVE (FIRENZE). 326/FI

ANTINORI

DENOMINAZIONE DI ORIGINE CONTROLLATA

Fattorie dei
Marchesi L. e P. Antinori

Imbottigliato alle Cantine Antinori - S. Casciano V.P. (382 FI)

CONT. NETTO Lt. 0,720
3/4 QUART

GRADI ALCOOL 12,5
ALCOHOL 12,5% BY VOL.

IMPORTED

LUGANA

WHITE WINE

RUFFINO

NET CONTENTS
1 PINT 8 FL. OZ.

SCHIEFFELIN & CO. - NEW YORK
IMPORTERS SOLE U.S.
SINCE 1794 DISTRIBUTORS

ALCOHOL BY
VOLUME 11½%

FONTANA CANDIDA

MARCHIO DEPOSITATO

FRASCATI SUPERIORE

VINO A DENOMINAZIONE DI ORIGINE CONTROLLATA
PRODUCED & BOTTLED by VINI DI FONTANA CANDIDA S, p. A. - FRASCATI
IN THE PRODUCTION ZONE
MONTEPORZIO CATONE - ITALY

Crosse & Blackwell Vintage Cellars
SOLE AGENT   NEW YORK, N.Y
N.Y - 1 - 475
Net contents 1 Pint 8 Fl. Oz   PRODUCT OF ITALY   Alcohol 12% by volume

bor Valpolicella, by contrast, as the red you would choose if the weather grew unexpectedly cooler. They both come from the same grapes grown in adjacent regions, but the Valpolicella, because of soil differences, has more flavor and a deeper cherry color. Neither should be considered candidates for aging.

Chianti is clearly the next step on the scale. If you want to make this a two-step process, you can interpose a *fiaschi* if you can still find any. They are those youthful Chiantis that come in the straw-covered jugs, but they are not necessary to study here and, besides, they will have their share of the limelight in the Chianti section. Choose instead a Chianti Classico (one that comes from the central region) or Chianti Classico Vecchio, which is a medium-bodied wine. A bit heavier would be a Grumello, Inferno or a Sassella. They all come from subdistricts of Lombardy. All are made from the Nebbiolo grape, and are among the finest wines of Italy. They tend to be dry and slightly tannic, thus bitter in youth and better in age.

Next are the heavyweights, both in terms of body and class. A Chianti Riserva is one that has spent additional time in wood and afterward was cellared longer than usual. This is the best of the breed, and almost always a nice bottle. From farther north, in the foothills of the Alps, come Barbaresco, Ghemme, Gattinara and Spanna. These can be classed together just behind Barolo, which is widely considered the finest of them all. There are qualitative differences among them. Gattinara, probably second only to Barolo, is elegant and round; Ghemme may be next with its violet scent; and last—but still excellent—is Barbaresco, slightly lighter in body, soft and delicate. Spanna is just another local name for the Nebbiolo grape from which they are all made. Spanna on the label means it comes from the outlying areas surrounding a town such as Gattinara, and can't be called by the town name itself. Gattinara is grown on the hillsides, Spanna, further down the slope. And then there is Barolo—same grape—same region—but the best. This is the wine that wins respect from French oenophiles. A fine old bottle of Barolo (and they are available if you look) is an excellent wine. Its power is such that the tradition in Piedmont, where it is made, is to leave some of it out to air for twenty-four hours before serving it to a special guest. The slight oxidation is supposed to give the wine a certain lift. Barolos have a hard, garnet color, and are deeply scented, but with age they gain a velvet texture and a lovely balance.

We cannot end on Barolo, no matter how good it is. That would ignore Brunello di Montalcino and the type of wines called Amarones. These are the whoppers. Brunello is the most aristocratic wine. It is rare in this country, very rare, but not impossible to find. It is high in alcohol (at least 12½%) and that helps account for its body, and for its near-legendary ability to age. The grape is the Sangiovese, similar to the one that dominates its neighbor Chianti. The wines here are aged much longer; from four to six years in wood. They consequently develop a greater fullness, more flavor and of course tannin. It is natu-

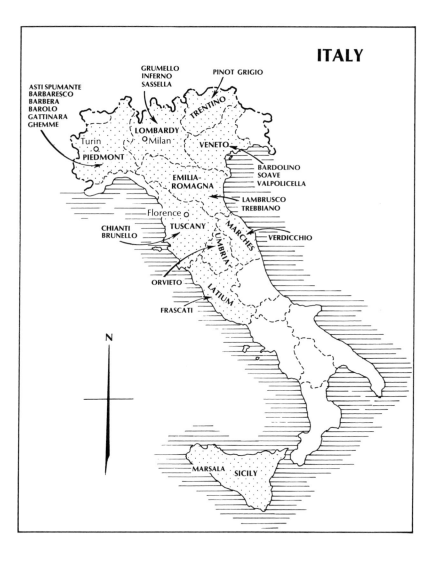

ITALY

rally a very intense wine, and contemporary bottles have labels advising the buyer to open the wine a day prior to serving.

The other type of wine is the Amarone. These wines are made in the Veronese region by a unique process. The grapes are picked quite late when completely ripe. After harvest, the ripe grapes are laid on racks in sheds to dry until some of their moisture has evaporated and they have become berry-like. This concentrates their flavor and gives them unusual intensity. As might be expected, they have a raisin taste and a complementary hot, slightly bitter finish. They also have a very high alcohol level, often over fourteen percent. In all, they are extremely powerful, huge-bodied and intense dry wines which can live a long time.

Preferred:	
light:	Bardolino
medium:	Valpolicella
	Chianti Classico
	Grumello
heavy:	Barbaresco
	Barolo
whoppers:	Brunello
	Amarone
Alternatives:	
medium:	An Inferno, Sassella or Spanna for the Grumello
heavy:	A Barbera D'Asti for the Barbaresco
	A Gattinara or Ghemme for the Barolo
Optional:	A Chianti fiaschi—those round bottles
Vintages:	Any vintage is acceptable for the lighter-bodied wines. However, age improves all the others, so try hard to find ones that are at least five years old. Conforming the vintages is not important.

Consumerism. The quality of France's better wines is known almost to a decimal point, but Italy is relatively unexplored territory for the wine adventurer—it is rife with finds, especially in the north, where the hill country near the Alps produces Italy's finest wines. As we press pariahs turn our spotlights of publicity on them, their prices will escalate, but for now there are better bargains there than anywhere. A 1967 Spanna can be found in New York in the three dollar range. Ten-year-old Gattinaras are not uncommon for under five dollars. Only a rare twenty-year-old Barolo will fetch significantly more. These are all complex, robust wines, and a steal at their current prices!

We have already covered the fact that "classico" on a label means that the wine comes from the center of the growing area. Another term you may encounter is "superiore," which means that the grapes must have yielded a higher alcoholic content and that—by implication—the wine is superior. Depending upon the region, the wines will also have to have met other higher standards.

In tasting the wines you will notice that many of them, especially the heavier ones, have a tarry, bitter finish. This makes them good for food but not entirely pleasant for sipping unaccompanied. Be warned that it is nice to have cheese nearby. Incidentally, there is an old postulate in the wine trade: "Buy on bread; sell on cheese." Bread is neutral and clears the palate. Cheese makes everything taste better.

TASTING 14: Italian Whites—A Disunited View

It is more difficult to talk about Italian whites because—unlike the reds—there is no single theme that unites them. After dividing them into sweet wines and dry wines you still have three subcategories of dry: The soft, the light, and the medium-bodied mellow wines. Even these are imperfect distinctions. Personally I don't think it is necessary to go into detail because—again, unlike Italian red wines—the whites never really rise to distinction. Most are simple wines for simple drinking: worthy of attention but not idolatry. Their selling point is their refreshing taste and the charm with which they accompany seafood. At their worst—and a few bad Italian whites do get to this country—they contain some off tastes, such as that of roasted sesame seeds, or they may be just plain dull.

The number of Italian whites that need concern us is small: Frascati, Verdicchio, Soave, Pinot Grigio and the unusual one, Orvieto. It is best to start with Frascati—excellent to start with Frascati—providing the wine is impeccably fresh. Within a year of the date on the label, it is sure to be clean, with a hint of nuts and wood, dry and crisp with almost no aftertaste. It can be a treacherous wine, because it is so easy to sip and the alcohol may go unnoticed . . . but not for long. I recently have had an excellent example in the Fontana Candida imported by Crosse & Blackwell.

A Verdicchio might seem to have a trifle more substance and more delicacy. It too is an appetizing wine, and its slight ending bitterness makes it best with seafood. In the same breath you can add Soave. Again we have a wine noted for its agreeableness, its youthfulness and its ability to complement that which swims. It might be the grape blend, it might be its northern origin, but once more there is a slight increase in the weight of the wine.

To change styles seek out a Pinot Grigio. It is not as well known a wine as the foregoing. Like most crisp wines it is aromatic, and when well made it has a hint of spice. It should have more character than the other light-bodied whites. To me it seems akin to a German wine but without the sweetness.

The white with the most character is Orvieto. There are two types. Let us call them dry and mellow. It is the mellow, or Orvieto Abboccato, that is of the most interest. The grapes are vinified slowly and contain some "noble rot." Then they spend a longer time in wood than is usual for a white. Although the wine is fermented totally dry, a little intensely rich liquor is added at the end. The result is a tart wine with a good residual sugar balance, and more individuality than any of the others.

Preferred:
light-bodied: Frascati (Fontana Candida)
Soave
crisp: Pinot Grigio
mellow: Orvieto Abboccato
Alternatives:
light-bodied: Verdicchio for Soave
mellow: Corvo

Consumerism. Excluding Orvieto, the major attractions of Italian white wine should be their freshness and their price. Look for the youngest, two years old at the maximum, and don't overspend. Also be prepared for a lack of consistency.

Chianti

The best way to explore Italian wines in depth is to stick with a single region. The most accessible of all is Chianti. Everything that is right and wrong in Italian wines can be found in bottles bearing this label.

Chianti is an invented, or at least a created, wine. Like Champagne, whose perfection we credit to one man, Chianti in its present form was developed by Baron Bettino Ricasoli in the 1870s. He was a man of considerable talents, an aristocrat and one of Italy's first prime ministers. True to the stereotype of national character, he also had a jealous temperament. He was not handsome, so the story goes, and retired to his hereditary family seat in rural Tuscany to forestall any potential impropriety on the part of his young and beautiful wife. To occupy his time usefully he improved his vineyards and developed a blend of four grapes—which is what Chianti is today. The four are Sangiovese (50–80%), which is obviously the dominant; the Trebbiano (10–30%), actually a white grape; the Malvasia (10–30%) for weight and a certain sweetness; and the Canaiolo (10–30%). If you perversely total my figures that could add up to 170%, and that doesn't include up to five percent of other grapes that can legally be used.

Chianti is not Italy's best wine, just its most popular. Because of this popularity, the word Chianti was long abused. Growers from the Alps to the Appian Way put their red wines in jugs and called it Chianti. Because of laws first passed in 1924 and more stringently enforced by presidential decree #930 in 1963 (which established the D.O.C. mechanism), the name can only be used for wine coming from Tuscany, the only place that real Chianti was ever produced.

The most famous Chianti is labeled "classico." It comes from the central Tuscany region between Florence and Siena. Those wines coming from near Florence have more bouquet. Those coming from closer to Siena are higher in alcohol. Chianto Classico is not the best region;

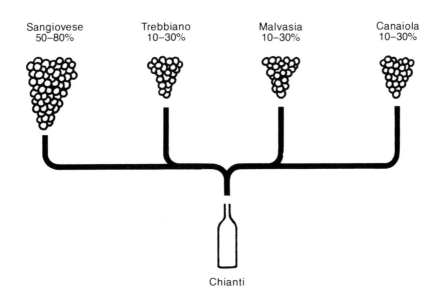

Sangiovese 50–80% Trebbiano 10–30% Malvasia 10–30% Canaiola 10–30%

Chianti

others are good, as well. There is Chianti Rufina and Chianti Montalbano and others as well. Originally the regions tried to distinguish themselves by putting little labels with heraldic signs around the bottle's neck. There were centaurs, bunches of grapes or lilies in gold and red. It became a code that only the cognoscenti could break. The major producers withdrew entirely from this form of labeling, reasoning that their names were more famous. They were right. Also other people were using the *consorzi* regional labels to bottle mediocre wine and so to some extent the labels lost their worth as guarantees of superior quality.

Ignoring the district of origin, there are still three distinctly different styles of Chianti. For convenience it is easiest to divide them into those meant to be drunk young and those meant to age. The young wines have an appeal similar to a Beaujolais. They are fresh, fruity and prickly with acidity. The slight frothiness comes from the use of the "governo" technique. After the original wine has fermented additional, unfermented grape "must" is added. That starts it fermenting again. Malic acid, which is rather harsh to the taste, converts to the softer lactic acid, and the wine picks up a slight bubbly edge. In its lightest form one drinks it where it is made. Slightly stronger, more earthy but still fresh is the wine bottled in straw-covered fiaschi. These are the bowling-ball-shaped covered jugs that once were ubiquitous. Their shape should be a clear indication that they are meant to be consumed young, for with a shape like that they are too unwieldy to stack and age. You should drink them within a year before their freshness and fruitiness dissipate. *Fiaschi* are disappearing; the cost of covering the bottle in straw has come perilously close to equalling the cost of the wine. The same wine will probably be marketed with a plastic cover or some other form of identification and be quite as unpretentiously enjoyable.

The more ambitious Chianti is easiest to recognize by its "claret-style" bottle. The wine is more complex and has more to offer. The grapes used will probably be superior. There is no softening second fermentation, and the wine will have spent more time in oak before being bottled; the minimum is two years. Wines with three years of aging in oak and sometimes two more in the bottle are entitled to label themselves "Riserva." These, especially the Classico Riservas, have the most potential for improvement when laid down. In contrast, the typical tavern Chianti usually is aged only six months.

Because Chiantis are blends of four grapes, they are very much subject to stylistic variations. It is difficult to generalize about them, but if you find an eight-year-old Chianti it may remind you of a lean Burgundy because of its earthy quality and forward fragrance. The wood may make it appear drier and, as is usual in northern Italian wines, there may be a hint of tar or iodine with a typical lightly bitter finish. These tend to be emphatic wines, more gutsy than refined.

Aside from the style of the wine, the quality will naturally vary from year to year in accordance with the weather. Weather is more regular in Italy than it is for its northern neighbors. The quality of the vintages will vary but not nearly so radically as in France or Germany. There have been some outstanding years, 1971 was one, but overall there is a general consistency. The years are meaningful but by the time you have specialized enough in Italian wines to want to lay some bottles away, you will already have gotten a feeling for the trend of the vintages.

TASTING 15: Italian Wines—Chiantis

The quality levels of Chiantis are so neatly broken up that our tasting is obvious: A *fiasco*, a regular Classico, and a Riserva. Much of the information we get about these Chiantis we receive indirectly. The labels will tell you where the wine was made, but not its quality or its style. As we know, we glean that from the bottle shape: *Fiaschi* for wines to be drunk young, Bordeaux-type bottle for the finer wines.

Preferred:
    Fiasco: Any still available on American market
    Classico: Villa Antinori; Bertolli; Ruffino
    Riserva: Brolio Riserva; Melini
Alternatives:
    Fiasco: Any but be sure it is fresh, not stale stock
    Classico: Any of the better producers
    Riserva: Any of the better producers

Consumerism. The prime denominator of quality in Chianti is not locale, but the name of the maker. Usually this is one of the large wine houses or cooperatives such as Ricasoli, Frescobaldi, Melini, Ruffino or Antinori. The large shipping and producing houses have a deservedly high reputation. Their names are so important that the best houses use Chianti only as the second name, relying instead on their own personal brands to identify their finest products. An example of such a wine would be the Brolio Riserva, the top wine from the Ricasoli family. The words "Chianti Classico" appear in only small letters on the label, almost as an afterthought.

VINTAGE CHART OF ITALIAN WINES

RED WINES	'61	'62	'63	'64	'65	'66	'67	'68	'69	'70	'71	'72	'73	'74	'75	All-time greats
Amarone di Valpolicella	8a	8a	7a	10a	6a	8a	8a	8a	9a	7a	8a	7a	8a	9a	9a	
Barbaresco	9b	8b	2e	10	6b	2e	8a	6c	7a	8a	10	2d	6c	9a	5a	
Barbera	8b	8b	4e	9	6b	2e	7a	6c	7a	8a	10	2d	5c	8a	5a	
Bardolino	6	9	6	8	6	6	7	7	9	7	8	5	7	7	8a	1957
Barolo	10b	8b	4e	10	8b	2e	8a	6c	7a	8a	10	2d	6c	9a	5a	1947-1958
Brunello di Montalcino	6d	—	—	10a	6c	7c	8a	6b	7b	10a	10a	4d	6c	6b	10a	1945-1955
Cabernet Trentino	6d	4d	6d	10a	2d	6d	6d	4d	10b	10b	8b	4c	4c	4c	6a	1947-1949-1959
Castel del Monte	6d	4d	4d	4d	10d	8d	6d	10d	8d	6d	6d	6d	8a	8b	8a	1951
Chianti	4e	8c	2e	6cʳ	4c	4c	6b	8b	8b	8a	8a	4d	4c	8b	8	
Chianti Classico	4	8c	2e	8c	6c	6c	8b	8b	8b	8a	10a	4d	4c	8b	8	
Frecciarossa	—	—	—	—	6	6	10	8	10	10	8	4	8	8	6	
Gattinara	8b	6b	2e	10	6b	4e	6a	8c	8a	8a	4	2d	4c	10a	6a	1952
Ghemme	6d	8b	2e	8	2d	2e	6a	4e	6a	8b	8	6d	8c	10a	6a	1947
Inferno	8d	4e	—	10	2e	4e	6c	4c	8b	8b	8a	4a	6a	4a	6a	1947-1952
Lambrusco di Sorbara	10e	2e	6e	2e	4e	2e	4e	6e	6e	8a	10a	4a	6a	6a	8a	
Merlot Trentino	8d	6d	2d	8a	2d	6d	6d	4d	10b	6d	8b	2d	2c	6c	4a	1947-1959
Pinot Nero Alto Adige	—	—	—	—	2d	6d	4d	6b	10b	4d	8b	4d	6c	6c	4a	
Santa Maddalena	—	—	—	—	2d	6d	6d	8b	8b	4d	8b	8c	6c	8b	8a	
Sassella	8d	4e	4e	—	2e	4e	6c	4c	8b	8b	8a	4a	6a	4a	6a	1947-1952
Sfurzat	—	4e	4e	10	2e	4e	6c	4c	6	8b	8a	4a	6a	4a	6a	1947-1952
Torgiano	7	8	7	9	—	8	6	10	6	10	8	8	6	6	4	1948
Valpolicella	6	8c	2e	8	6	7	8	7	8	8	9	8	8	7	8a	1947-1952
Vino Nobile di Montepulciano					2e	6c	10b	8b	8b	10a	4a	4d	8c	6b	10	1958
WHITE WINES																
Etna Bianco					8	6	8	8	2	8	4	4	6	6	4	1954
Frascati					5	6	9	8	7	7	7	4	6	8	7	
Lugana					4	4	4	4	8	6	6	6	6	8	4	
Orvieto					—	—	—	—	—	6	8	4	8	8	6	
Pinot dell'Oltrepò					6	6	8	6	6	10	8	2	6	6	4	1947-1958
Soave					8	10	8	7	8	8	9	7	8	7	8	
Trebbiano di Romagna					6	6	6	6	4	10	8	6	6	8	8	1956-1957
Velletri Castelli Romani					4	6	9	8	7	7	7	3	6	8	7	1946
Verdicchio					6	2	4	6	4	6	6	4	6	2	6	1958

KEY TO READING TABLE: 2: less than average vintage. 4: average vintage. 6: good vintage. 8: very good vintage. 10: exceptional vintage.

Additional qualifications are indicated by the letters a), b), c), d), e) : a) : best with further aging. b) : can improve with further aging. c) : ready for drinking. d) : caution advised if aged further. e) : wine may be too old to drink.

The right-hand column lists the all-time great vintages, which all rate ten points.

Copyright © 1977 Italian Wine Promotion Center

The standard Classico is frequently a good buy. It may not cost significantly more than a fiasco. In comparison to wines of other countries in a similar price range, Chianti is again a superior value. The Riservas are nicely aged, well made and sophisticated at a reasonable price.

Last, Italian wines in general and Chiantis in particular are prone to finding their way into someone's bargain bin. *Fiaschi* don't last long, so beware. Beware also of unknown producers. Many reputable producers may happen to be unfamiliar to us, but using an unknown name *is* the most frequent means of selling poor wine. Deal with a wine merchant who has stock in depth and high turnover. Ask him if the wine is good; an honest man will tell you if some bottles are risky. Be sure you can return any bad bottles.

To my knowledge, the following chart is the only one of its kind. It was compiled by the Italian Trade Commission, and friends there have kindly lent it to me.

It is not all-inclusive. It accents those wines which are generally available in the United States, and its judgments reflect what happened to the average wine in that region in that year. Some wines may be better made than others, some may last longer. Rely on your own palate.

THE UNITED STATES

Jugs made it all happen. They popularized wine and separated it from its myth. There can be no snobbery associated with a jug wine, no intimidating connoisseur, no ritualistic pouring, no Omar Khayyam-esque phrases. Instead it's plastic cups and ice cubes. Good. Jugs have done their job of education. Americans are not afraid of wine any more. They are becoming adventuresome and more demanding, so a new industry has emerged. The California premium and boutique wineries are capturing the headlines with their challenges to the French bastions of quality and on the way are raising the public's perception of American wines. We are breaking our dependence on Europe, saying that we can do great things here. With jingoistic pride, aging English actors are hired by large wineries to proclaim that American wines are among the finest anywhere.

The question is, which American wines? We have the right to be proud of our wines. They have come from almost nowhere and in the span of two decades have gained international recognition. A few vineyards in a few vintages have succeeded in turning out brilliant wines. However, it is nonsense to say that all California or domestic wines are superior. There are excellent wines in both bulk and premium, but there is at least as much to be avoided as well.

American vineyards are infants compared to those of Europe, and it will take more than a few years to establish their real quality. Château Ausone in Bordeaux was cultivated when the Roman poet Ausonious lived there. Schloss Vollrads dates from Charlemagne's time. Italian and Burgundian vineyards are even older. Still, there is no special value that accrues to time itself. What is important, however, is the tedious perfecting by trial and error of the best sites and micro-climates. The reason that California has progressed so far so quickly is because scientists have learned which grapes prosper in which climates. Their advice is still inexact. They can tell where a grape will grow but not its ultimate quality. That involves soil substructure, drainage, extended weather patterns and other components too complex even for the most elaborate regression analysis. In the end, the only way to see what type of wine will be produced is to grow it over a long period of time and see what comes of it.

The California wine industry, in truth, has existed only since the repeal of Prohibition—under half a century. Prohibition drove the best winemakers out of the country and caused the best vineyards to be plowed under. The only grapes grown during this period were for eating, plus a limited amount for home wine-making and sacramental wines. Our legacy from Prohibition has been grape varieties which are not suitable for wine: Thick skins, poor flavor, but exportable. Through the 1940s and 1950s it was almost impossible to get more than a dollar a bottle for American wine, so there was no incentive to upgrade them. A few men, however, were always experimenting. When vines grew old they would replace them with premium varieties. They used better technology. They gained experience, and around them a cluster of enthusiastic consumers gathered. The real wine boom which brought money, attention and skill and which upgraded all wines dates only from 1966. Very, very few of the premium-wine producers of today were around ten years ago. These newcomers are still feeling their way. Their styles are not yet set. Their wines are variable. It will not be the same in any two years. In other words, it will be a few more years before the industry has evolved enough to make specific judgments on its validity.

What you can say as a start is that you can divide the field into jugs and nonjugs. The jugs, or bulk wines are by and large disappointing. They may be soundly made but more often they are characterless and slightly sweet. They are aimed at an audience that prefers blandness, and much of their appeal lies in their inexpensiveness. There are a few exceptions to this rule of low quality; it takes background and ability to taste to find them. This is where your studies will begin to pay off. We will mention some of the exceptions later in this chapter.

American wines are divided into two types: Varietal and generic. A *varietal* wine is made from one variety of grapes,* and is named for that *variety* (e.g., Pinot Noir, Cabernet Sauvignon or Zinfandel). A *generic* wine is named after a region or place (e.g., "Pink Chablis," "Hearty Burgundy" or "Mountain Red"), never a grape. *A varietal wine will nearly always be superior to a generic.* A generic wine is a blend. The place name of a generic wine is meaningless. "Hearty Burgundy" does not mean that a wine tastes like a Burgundy or even was made from the Pinot Noir grape, which is the *only* grape permitted to be used in real French Burgundy. It is just a nice commercial name that people associate with quality. Such generic wines may be blends of up to thirty different grapes. The purpose is to standardize production so as to produce a uniform taste. The grapes they use, such as Thompson Seedless or Carignane, produce three to four times as much wine per acre of land as a premium grape would, but with a proportionate loss of character. It takes luck and an exceptional winemaker to turn these ingredients into something more than a *vin ordinaire*—but it does happen.

Generic wines make for good drinking but they are seldom good wine. That area is reserved for varietals. Some varietals are in a similar low price bracket, but most command a premium because they are more expensive to produce. For the most part, the grapes for the varietal wines are grown in the cooler valleys surrounding San Francisco, as opposed to the hot Central Valley of Southern California, where the more prolific grape varieties are grown. The cooler climate permits the grapes to ripen more slowly, draw more flavor from the soil and develop a better acid-sugar balance.

Confining ourselves to California wines ignores the other major wine area of the United States: The lovely Finger Lakes region of New

---

* Actually a percentage of other varieties are permitted to be added but the character of the lead grape predominates.

York State. With one notable exception (Dr. Konstantin Frank) and a few other pioneers, there are no fine wines grown here. The wines of Taylor and the sparkling wines of Great Western taste odd because they use an entirely different species of grape from any we've encountered so far. It is an important difference. All California wines are made from grapes descended from European vines (v. vinifera). New York wines are made from native American stock (v. labrusca) which is heartier and can withstand the cold upstate winters. V. labrusca wines will taste muskier, with an overtone of thick wild fruit grapes. They call this taste "foxy," though I can't figure out why. Such is the foolishness of some wine terms, but then again I've never tasted a New York State fox. To be more practical, if you are familiar with Concord Grape Jelly, that is a related grape.

TASTING 16: American Wines

The simplest and most beneficial tasting would be to take a look at an all-American favorite like Almaden Mountain Red or Gallo Hearty Burgundy and then compare it to some varietal wine. These generics represent the most popular qualities of jug wines. They are widely known; people can feel comfortable with them. They are widely available. And they are inexpensive. The question is, will you enjoy the varietal more, and will it be worth the extra money to you?

	red	*white*
Preferred:		
generic:	Almaden Mountain Red	Inglenook Chablis
	Gallo Hearty Burgundy	
varietal:	Inglenook Zinfandel	Los Hermanos Chardonnay
Alternatives:		
generic:	Mondavi Red Table Wine	Mondavi White Table Wine

Consumerism. Generic wines are for people who don't know or don't care about wine. They are a holdover from a time when the wine industry thought the consumer had to be patronized and led. Their importance is fading. It is much better to know what grape your wine is made from. You will have a clearer idea of what to expect and any additional money should yield you a much more enjoyable wine.

VI

SOPHISTICATION

Grapes are probably the most sensitive fruit in cultivation. While some people may argue the merits of California avocados versus those of Florida, in wine it is not a matter of thousands of miles but of a few feet that may make the difference. In the long run, cyclical climatic variations cancel themselves out, and it is the nature of the soil that most influences the taste of the wine. The composition of the earth varies continuously, so that a short distance can mean a radical alteration.

Individual wines are a relatively recent phenomenon. In ancient times, when wines were carried in metal flasks because glass was too expensive, only wines from such broad areas as Médoc, Graves or Palus were known. A thin film of oil was floated over the wine's surface to prevent it from oxidizing, because corks hadn't been invented yet. Under such conditions, quality had no chance to develop or be discerned. It was only as growers learned how to control fermentation, and as the merits of glass and cork began to be appreciated, that little by little the uniqueness of the individual communes and then of specific vineyards became apparent.

The reason wine regions developed was because they produced wines which shared certain characteristics. They had a common style. This style is not one thing. You can't reduce it to a formula. Instead it is a fuzzy locus of points. You don't know precisely where it starts, but at some point it has substance. Médoc, for instance, makes an identifiable type of wine, but each château is a variation on the theme and not the theme itself. Much of the interest of wine is in these variations, but first it would be best to get acquainted with the 'general characteristics of the major regions.

BORDEAUX

Ask anyone to name a prestigious wine, and if he can name one at all it will be a Bordeaux. History has given Bordeaux the fame, nature has given it the quality, and fortune has given it the volume to support its myth. It produces more wine than anywhere else in France, and fortunately there are enough great wines grown there for some to appear on any restaurant's cellar list.

As you are aware by now, Bordeaux is subdivided into four major regions. The classic area of the famous châteaux is west of the River Gironde and includes Haut-Médoc and Graves. Graves in turn encompasses Barsac and Sauternes, but since these two produce sweet white wines, they will be considered elsewhere. The areas to the east are St.-Emilion and Pomerol. Adjacent areas also produce wine but aren't nearly as famous.

There is a clear difference in style between the wines on opposing sides of the river. Weather, soil and all the other factors we've covered play their part, but the simplest explanation is that different grapes are used. The Médoc and Graves rely heavily on Cabernet Sauvignon (Cabernet) while St.-Emilion and Pomerol favor Merlot. Because of

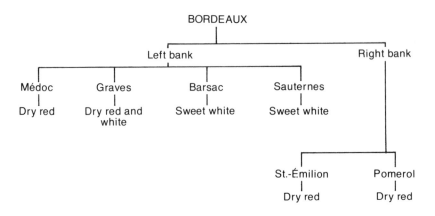

the nature of the Cabernet grapes, wines from the western shore will be harder, more tannic and will live longer. They also mature more slowly. In contrast wines from the east will be more mellow and supple and easier to drink when young.

The wines of the Haut-Médoc, which the English during their 300-year occupation of the area called "claret," naturally became the criteria against which all other wines are judged. Their long life and natural hard aristocracy (based on tannin) is in contrast to the gentler style of the St.-Emilions and Pomerols. Because of this some people say the latter are like Burgundies, but that accepts the false logic of "because you are not like me, you are like something else."

It is dangerous to generalize about wines from one area. Wine tends not to be homogeneous but, rather, extremely varied. A wine of one

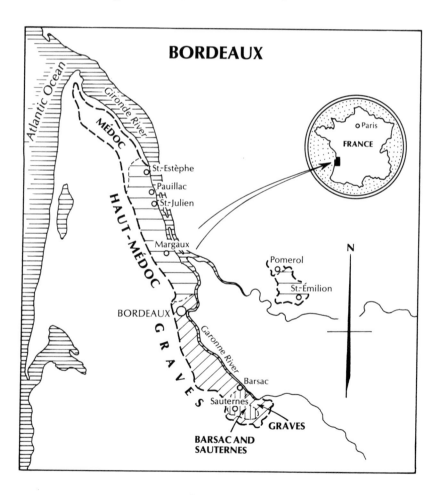

region might have more in common with another region than it does with its nearest neighbor. What allows us to generalize impetuously is that the typical wine will hold certain characteristics even though no one wine may be precisely typical. What doubles the hazard is that, additionally, all wines will vary with each new vintage. Having admitted the impossibility of quantifying the unquantifiable, we will now recklessly go ahead and do precisely that. We start by getting clear the tastes of the subregions.

The Haut-Médoc and Graves— The Left Bank

What should you expect from the wines of Haut-Médoc and Graves? Well, that depends on which one you've chosen to try. As you will see in the next tasting, not only do the two subregions differ, but Médoc varies quite a bit within itself.

In the Haut-Médoc, *the northern parishes are harder, the southern are more mellow.* Still, what they share is that powerful Cabernet nose and a deep purple color. The bouquet should hint at wood (or old cigar boxes), tannin and dark, heavy berries such as black currants mixed with flowers (some say violets, but being a city boy I'm less specific). The taste will be dry and mouth-filling, confirming the presence of the wood and, hopefully, fruit. Good Haut-Médocs are almost like wine concentrate. They have more of everything. They are that powerful. If the wine is young, look for that fruit, even if it is hidden under tannin. Without fruit, to my mind, the Médocs are unredeemable savages. They have astringency without grace. Finally, the wine should have a long and complex finish.

All Bordeaux wines tend to be austere, perhaps *Graves* more than most. The wine is like the soil. The subsurface contains quartzite over layers of loam and clay interspersed with lime and ferrous sand. It is similar to the soil of the Rheingau, and a subtle similarity of taste may become apparent to a very experienced taster. The main differences will come from the different climate and grapes. The roots of the vines of Graves grow deep and bring to the grape a dry earthiness which in its better moments yields an intense fruit bouquet. The city of Bordeaux is located in the center of Graves, and that accounts for the scarcity of reds grown thereabouts. The most accessible land has been claimed by the creeping suburbs. The great Château Haut-Brion is virtually surrounded by city.

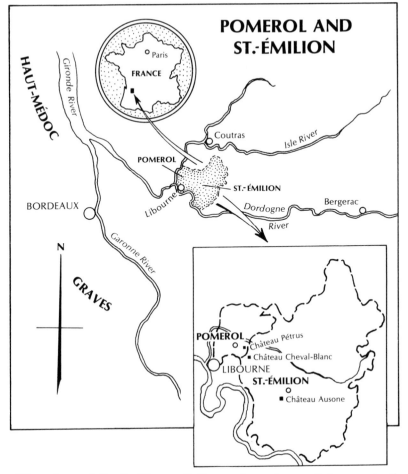

The wines of *St.-Emilion* and *Pomerol* are less well known to the public than those of the Médoc. With only three top exceptions, their popularity is a post-war phenomenon. Names like Châteaux Pétrus, Ausone or Cheval-Blanc and a sprinkling of others may be familiar, but by and large people do not make the Herculean effort to familiarize themselves with these individual estates as they do with the three-score grand crus of the Haut-Médoc. This is a shame, because many of the wines here are less expensive and quite as appealing as their neighbors across the river.

The dominant grape* here is Merlot, which shares some of the same

* Remember that all Bordeaux are blends, and that when I say that there is one dominant grape, it usually comprises seventy to ninety percent of the wine.

taste characteristics as Cabernet Sauvignon but is relatively lighter, softer and richer. It is quicker to ripen and once bottled, faster to mature. Because its growing season is shorter, it is less prey to fall frosts and rains. If the summer is a slow, cool one, its berries are still more capable of full ripening than other varieties. This means that in years when other grapes are affected by the bad climate, Merlot *may* still have the potential to make a superior wine. Theoretically there should be fewer bad bottles from Pomerol than from the Haut-Médoc in that type of year.

The maturity rate of a Pomerol or a St.-Emilion is different from that of a Médoc. A common benchmark in the trade is that a poor vintage should be ready in four years while a successful one may require a decade or more.

Although St.-Emilion and Pomerol are contiguous, their soil and wines contrast. You will find that Pomerols are lighter of body and more metallic than a St.-Emilion and have a decidedly fuller aroma; St.-Emilions are notably low on bouquet. That is something to keep in mind when trying to identify one in a blind tasting. Both areas will show a softness when compared to a Médoc, but the Pomerol should be the richer and riper, with a higher glycerine content that fills the mouth.

Another contrast to the Médocs is their method of organizing and classifying their wines. Neither Pomerol nor St.-Emilion are broken down into communes like the Médoc. Only St.-Emilion has an official ranking of its wines and that only came about as recently as 1955.

Pomerol has no ranking whatsoever, although there is a general consensus on the relative merits of the various châteaux. Pétrus naturally comes first, is followed by Vieux-Château-Certan, Trotanoy, and others (if I continued the list, then the area would be classified). A personal favorite is Château Latour-Pomerol, but, in the spirit of this book: Don't let someone else tell you; know your own mind.

TASTING 17: Bordeaux Regions

Preferred:

Médoc	*Graves*	*St.-Émilion*	*Pomerol*
Ducru-Beaucail- lou	Pape-Clément Haut-Bailly	Figeac Gaffelière	Nenin L'Évangile
Léoville-Barton			

Alternatives:

Virtually any of	Any of the 12	Any of the 10	Since there is no
the 55 second-	classified red	premier	classification in
through fifth-	wines of	grand class	Pomerol I sug-
growth Grand	Graves ex-	wines exclud-	gest: Châteaux
Cru Classés	cluding	ing Château	Trotanoy,
but preferably	Ch. Haut	Ausone and	Gazin, Lafleur,
from St.-Julien	Brion and	Ch. Cheval	Certan-Giraud
	La Mission	Blanc	
	Haut Brion		

Vintages: All bottles tried should be from the same year. The following should provide the most accurate contrast:

General Characteristics

1967	A good year aging nicely . . . better in Pomerol and St.-Émilion.
1970	A superb harvest everywhere. Powerful with plenty of fruit.
1971	Another excellent year. Perhaps a touch lighter than 1970.
1973	A good drinkable year with huge quantity and light wines.
1975	Very young; expect hard, tannic wines.

If a bottle has a few years of age on it, more of the intrinsic style of the area will have had a chance to develop. The '75s and '76s might still be too young to be optimal.

Consumerism. It is an irony of inflation that some older vintages, such as 1967, 1970 or 1971 are available at the same prices as the 1975s. Favor these bargains. Also, for current drinking, the faster maturing wines of Pomerole and St.-Emilion are more pleasant than those of the Médoc, but all improve with age.

The Haut-Médoc

> "Many shall be restored that are now fallen
> and many shall fall that are now in honor."
> —Horace, *Ars Poetica*

Thus far we have compared separate regions; now let's look at something more subtle, the variations within a single region and their causes. The Haut-Médoc contains more fine vineyards than any other place on earth. Yet, from the north to the south these wines vary more from one another than they do as a group from a St.-Emilion or a Pomerol.

There is a theme that you will see recurring in all major wine regions: *Wines will change more from north to south than from east to west.* The distance need not be extreme; three to five miles will frequently do. As wines march northward in the Médoc, they pick up more acidity, color, tannin and have a bit less aroma. They become more masculine, hard and enduring. The same rule applies in Burgundy, and to some extent in Germany. In Napa and Sonoma the principle works in reverse. There, the cool regions are in the south near the ocean, while warm lands are inland toward the north. Wherever the styles of vinification are uniform, some variation of this rule will apply.

The other factor in the Haut-Médoc, as in all areas we've mentioned, is the composition of the soil. Its chemical makeup will influence the wine. This is a good thing to keep in mind while tasting. Silica, for instance, will produce a light wine with little alcohol and great delicacy. A high clay content will yield a deeper color, more tannin; robust and rather hard and alcoholic. Age will mellow that. The calcareous hillsides of the Haut-Médoc add bouquet. The ideal soil would be a balanced mixture of all these. Since soil content varies, the tastes from the different vineyards will vary, and more noticeable will be a character common to each of the communes.

Man, in his insatiable desire to create myth, seems to respect age in everything but himself. I personally do not favor Bordeaux that are much more than twenty years old. That seems to be about their peak considering that few vintages are great and wine is often mis-stored. Anything older is an interesting experiment in time but too damn risky for my pocketbook. But the general curiosity is not to be denied and who would turn down the opportunity to try an older wine. I own a few bottles from the nineteenth century that are sound and even two from the 1790s that I know are in perfect condition. However, the price of old wine is astronomical today and the only reason many of them are available is because their previous owners know they are fading or already dead.

Age in wine should not be valued for its own sake. It's like the question every diver is asked: "What is the farthest you've ever been down?" The question is meaningless; the light fades swiftly after about fifty feet and what is usually left is darkness, danger and pressure.

Old wines, however, can teach you very modern lessons. I learned one

from a bottle of 1900 Chateau Capbern that was given to me as a
birthday indulgence. If you don't recognize the name Capbern, don't
be surprised. It isn't even one of the 64 "grand cru" vineyards. It
occupies a place in that slightly lower rung of classification called "cru
bourgeois" and shows how unfair that rating can be to some proper-
ties. These "cru bourgeois" are also called "petits châteaux." The Capbern, when I opened it, was beautifully alive, fresh and sophisticated.
Any "petit château" that can last three-quarters of a century isn't too
"petit."

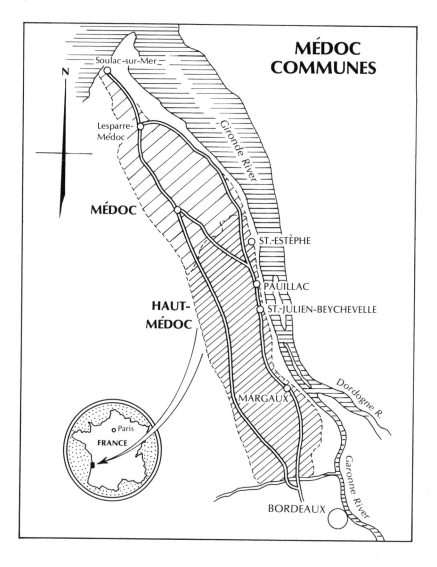

There is another lesson. Chateau Capbern is located in St. Estèphe, the most northerly of the communes in the Haut-Médoc. St. Estèphe has relatively few of the "grand crus" (only five) but many truly fine "petits chateaux" like Chateau Capbern. These are well worth searching out and are good values. The wines of St. Estèphe have their own style. They are weightier than those of the other communes. They are dense and have an earthy bouquet and, as demonstrated by the Capbern, have the potential of being very long lived.

There are no radical breaks dividing the communes. The vineyards of Cos-d'Estournel, which is in St.-Estèphe, are separated from those of Lafite in Pauillac by barely a footpath and a stone's throw, but the wines are vastly different. Could a few yards really mean so much?

Elsewhere perhaps, but here the difference is more artificial. Cos-d'Estournel uses up to eighty-five percent Cabernet Sauvignon, while Lafite lightens its style by using only sixty-six percent, of which about half might be Cabernet Franc. The soil is thus only one source of the variation. A closer comparison would be Mouton Rothschild, just down the road and also in Pauillac. Its wines are almost totally Cabernet Sauvignon. Nevertheless, Pauillac has its own unique style, and it must be quite successful because three of the five great growths and thirteen other grand crus come from there. This is obviously soil of distinction and there must be some common threads to its merits.

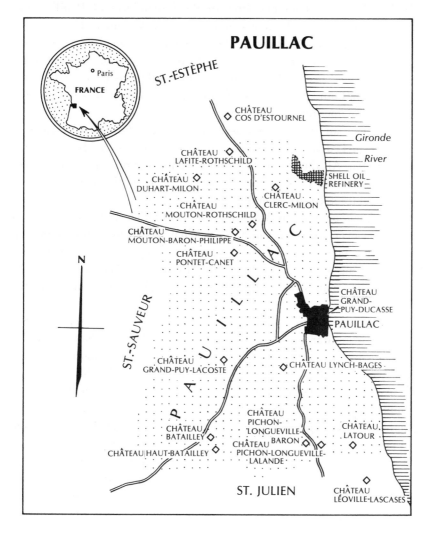

With each château trying to express its own individuality, it might seem a contradiction for themes to surface, but they do. Pauillac's wines have breed, a word easier to taste than to define. There is something in the wine that tells of ancient vines planted on a perfect site. There is a remarkable depth of flavor, compatible complexity and a perfume-like, fruit bouquet mounted on a velvet texture—that is, if the wine is mature. When the wine is young it can be a bear, but age mellows it. There is much more to be learned from Pauillac so we will return to it later.

The next commune is St.-Julien, the most representative of the Médoc. Its wines combine some of the forcefulness of Pauillac and St.-Estèphe with the lightness and finesse of Margaux. They have a deep, rich color and a lingering berry bouquet in good years. Even in poor years some of the estates seem to produce a wine more pleasant than could be expected. In my experience Léoville-Las-Cases and Ducru-Beaucaillou both show well in off vintages. Perhaps that is because the gravelly soil does not hold the rain.

I learned an interesting lesson here. Just before harvest time in 1970, I picked and tasted the ripe grapes in the fields of Ducru-Beaucaillou. All the complexity that I would recognize four years later in the bottle was present in that grape. The best winemaker does not add or subtract, he just liberates.

The final commune is Margaux. The land is flat and dull here, as it is almost everywhere in the Médoc. What passes for a hill is just an undulation taken too seriously. Without the mythology, the fields are as interesting as alfalfa, and yet the glad cries of visitors hang on the air. Oh how man loves to ascribe to the container the qualities of the contained.

The Médoc is quite small. Only about eleven miles separate St.-Estèphe from Margaux, but even in this short distance the terms we've used to describe the wines have grown progressively more feminine. The wines of Margaux are the most graceful of all. They are more delicate than powerful, are lighter rather than heavy-bodied, more supple than tannic. One thinks of perfume rather than just bouquet. In their best vintages the wines have a perfectly balanced concentration. In poor years, they can be thin and the tastes will fail to unite.

There is much talk around, and it's true, that great French wines require less aging and are lighter than they once were. At one time anyone who indulged in a claret of under fifteen years of age was said to be a child molester. But times change, and who has the money or patience to lay away a case for decades? New methods are employed now so that wines are drinkable younger and so that pundits can proclaim from Bordeaux that the 1973 edition of long-lived Mouton Rothschild is ready for drinking a scant four years after the harvest. Incidentally, these harpies are wrong. Light though it is, the Mouton needs years more, and to drink it now is small pleasure.

There have been five main changes in winemaking since the war:

- Modern grapes, particularly in Burgundy, are larger and so have a lower proportion of skin area, thus yielding less tannin and less color than smaller varieties would.
- The wines are not left on the skins as long, with the same effect on tannin and color: Less.
- During fermentation, the wine is no longer agitated over the crust of skins, pits and stems (which would give the wine more vigor).
- In the older days, some of the marc*—the extra juice pressed mechanically from the residual grape pulp after the free-run juice had been drawn off to make the wine—was reintroduced; it no longer is.
- Last, stems and stalks are no longer allowed to ferment with the wine, as in the past.

Not all these old processes were totally beneficial. Both the marc and the stalks are rather coarse stuff, but they did allow the wine to age and to pick up a number of attributes now absent.

Unless you drink some Bordeaux, all this writing has no meaning. You should try at least two but preferably three or four of the communes side by side. If you do this paired with the earlier Regional Tasting (10), then the St.-Julien you choose can do double duty. In any case, the same suggestions regarding identical vintages apply here. Any of the classified growths can be selected. It does not matter if a fourth growth is matched against a second: They both share very high quality. The odds are almost even that the lower-ranked wine can be the superior or that both are equal. The reason is that the rankings are based on the list compiled in 1855. That ranking today may suffice as a generalization, but it is inaccurate when taken as a specific order of merit.

At a minimum, one wine should be from St.-Estèphe and the other from St.-Julien or Margaux. This will show you the range, and accent the male/female playoff. One of the other things you will probably

---

* Marc also means brandy distilled from this second pressing.

notice is that the southern wine will appear more mature. A St.-Estèphe can take twenty to thirty percent longer to hit its peak.

TASTING 18: The Haut-Médoc

Preferred:

	Preferred	*Alternatives*
St.-Estèphe:	Cos-d'Estournel	Calon-Ségur
	Montrose	Phélan-Ségur
Pauillac:	Lynch-Bages	Pichon-Longueville-Baron
	Grand-Puy-Lacoste	Duhart-Milon
St.-Julien:	Ducru-Beaucaillou	Talbot
	Léoville-Barton	Gloria
Margaux:	Rausan-Ségla	Prieuré-Lichine
	Brane-Cantenac	La Lagune

Optional:

Pauillac:	Lafite Rothschild
	Mouton Rothschild
	Latour

Margaux:	Margaux

Vintages: See the vintage chart on page 28. Since these are all fine wines, try to get the maximum age you can. Also, for the preferred and alternative wines try to conform the vintage dates. This is not necessary, just useful. The premier grand cru optional wines can be taken from any year you can afford, but if it is an off year, expect to be sampling a ghost.

Consumerism. Before we leave Bordeaux this time, I want to make some observations which I think will be useful to you and help save you money.

I enjoy premier cru wines (Mouton Rothschild and its brothers) when served at other people's homes, but seldom at my own. I find my money better spent on three bottles of Cos-d'Estournel which I can buy for the same amount that it would cost to purchase one of its neighbor Lafite. Similarly, I prefer Pichon Lalande to Latour. Of course the wines are different. No one says they are the same, nor will anyone say that in any given year Cos will be inferior to Lafite. You are dealing in such stratospheres that both are superb wines. But people who do not know quality are bidding up the price of the premier cru wines because they feel that they must have the best even if they can't appreciate it. If the price break was twenty or thirty percent then I would play the field, but at two to three times the price, I know my own style. No wine rules should be rigid. I have a few Lafites, but I have cases of the others.

Another guide I use is when buying Bordeaux in any quantity, I choose best years. There isn't enough of a break between the poorest and the best vintages. A 1969 or a 1972 may cost only $1.50 less than a superb 1970 or 1971. I don't suggest we condemn the off years to eternal purgatory, but they will have to drop their prices to $3.00–$4.50 per bottle in order for them to be priced effectively. There are too many other fine Italian, California or Côte-du-Rhône wines that you can purchase for the price. So when a claret is good, it's worth the price. When it's not, it's worth very little.

Bordeaux have another problem associated with them. Aging . . . the thing that makes them great, is also their major drawback. You can grow old waiting for some of these wines to fully mature. So what can you do? You can drink them young, but if you are buying a good year and drinking it within five years of the vintage do not expect a developed wine with any finesse. Even ten years is too short for a big year like 1966, 1970, or 1975, although it will do for a good year like 1967. If you are going to buy fine wine, you must lay it away. Alternatively, if you are buying wines for present consumption, aim for those that will be ready soonest: St.-Emilions and Pomerols or those of the southern communes over a St.-Estèphe. Of course, less expensive but very good wines from the cru bourgeois will be ready sooner and they can be an attractive choice. Try not to drink wine too young. You are killing a potential work of art.

Lastly, not all the Bordeaux you face will come from a wine store. Many will be on restaurant wine lists. The practice is that the least expensive wine usually has the highest markup. So you will get your best value if you order a mid-range wine.

BURGUNDY

Which is better, Burgundy or Bordeaux; Beethoven or Brahms; Klee or Picasso? It's all meaningless. Let the Chevaliers du Tastevin fight the Commanderie du Bordeaux, but me, I'll sit on the sidelines and cry a blessing on both your cellars. I have no honor. I love the one I'm nearest.

Burgundy is in one sense easier to study—yet probably harder to understand—than Bordeaux. Here there is only one red wine grape worth studying, the noble Pinot Noir, which is never blended with anything else. But while grapes may never be mixed, owners are. Could you imagine Château Latour owned by sixty different families, each growing its own vines, harvesting on its own choice of days, vinifying in its own manner (in Limousin oak, American oak, old barrels, new barrels, then aging for two years or for three years) and bottling each under its own separate label, but all saying Château Latour? The wines

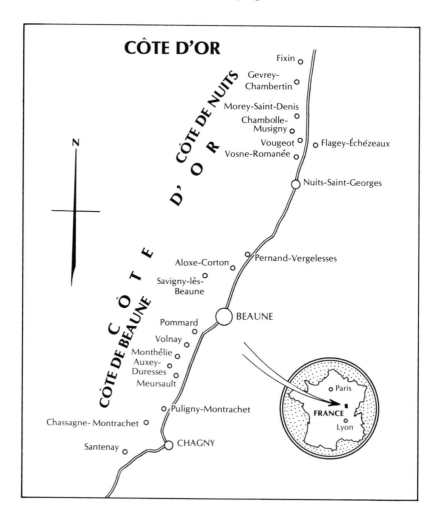

would vary more within themselves than they would with their neighbors. This is the situation in Burgundy. At least when you buy a specific château in Bordeaux you are buying a known quantity. In Burgundy, even if you know the vineyard there are still unanswered questions.

If I were to give a wine a human form, I would think of a great Bordeaux as a man six-foot-two or three, with a thirty-two-inch waist, aristocratic with white curly hair, an eighteenth-century gentleman, impeccably tailored, aloof, cold and unapproachable except in the best of company. Burgundies, by contrast, would appear as rich, rather tubby Dickensian characters with perpetual twinkles in their eyes and earth on their feet, and yet with the mind of a Byzantine courtier. Alternatively, and not in the least in contradiction, Burgundies can be like the greatest women: Beautiful, forty and wise.

The Golden Slope, the Côte d'Or, refers to all of contemporary Burgundy. The region is a scant thirty miles long and never very wide. It produces only a fraction of the amount of wine that Bordeaux is capable of, but the demand is as great. Hence the prices for its most famous vineyards humble even the most famous of the Haut-Médocs.

In the north the Côte d'Or is called the *Côte de Nuits,* named after the famous wine village, Nuits-St.-Georges. This practice of incorporating the most well-known vineyard name of an area into the title of a town is standard practice in Burgundy. The town of Vosne adds the name of its most renowned vineyard to become Vosne-Romanée. Gevrey becomes Gevrey-Chambertin, etc.

From the town of Corton on down, the overall region is named after the lovely city of Beaune, which is its heart, and is called the *Côte de Beaune.*

The Côte de Nuits, which is the northern section of the Côte d'Or, seems to have two personalities. In its north wines are male, big and

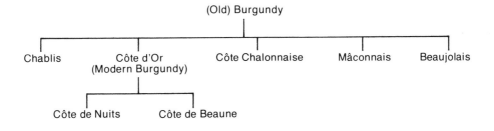

firm. They fill the mouth. They have a velvet texture and a bouquet-like ripe fruit in the summer sun. They also have an earthy quality that one learns to associate with "big" wines like those of the Côtes-du-Rhône, Northern Italy, and the California Petite Sirah, but here they have so much complexity and nuance that they stand a world apart.

The wines of the southern Côte de Nuits are unique. They are the quintessence of female sophistication: A bouquet of oriental opulence, a full mouth but so light it's like biting air, and a memory of elegance that endures. This, of course, is the wine at its best. A poor year there can be due to a lack of sun or too much rain. Without adequate sunlight the grapes fail to produce sufficient sugar. Then they do not have the fruity taste which is the grace of all wine. In this case, the vintner may chaptalize*—add sugar, which ferments to increase the alcohol. This is a common practice in Burgundy. It works when Nature does not. However, Nature does it best. Many producers (not all) had to resort to chaptalization in 1970, 1972, 1973, and 1974. The way I have found to detect it is to look for a very slight burnt taste in the middle of the mouth when sampling the wine. It is not obvious—it is quite subtle—but it adds nothing to the enjoyment of the wine.

One can study each town of Burgundy from Fixin in the north to Santenay in the extreme south. The travel books do it that way, but that is not our point here. We want trends, not just names. So what we do is cluster together several towns which share common characteristics. What is in the bottle is the truth, not what is on the label.

THE COTE DE NUITS

The first important town in the north is Fixin. Although the wine is unmistakably different, it stands in a similar relationship to its neighbors as St.-Estèphe does to the Haut-Médoc. Its wines are hearty and masculine, with more longevity and robustness than ones from farther south. They even have a more earthy tone. It became fashionable in the 1920s, when a well-regarded writer named Shrewsbury was around, to say these wines were slightly coarse. Fashion has perpetuated this anachronistic error. Powerful, yes; coarse, hardly.

---

* The practice of chaptalization, both legal and illegal, is more widespread than either producers or wine writers admit. It has occurred in most years in the seventies both in Bordeaux and Burgundy and regularly involved the well known as well as the obscure.

The next town is Gevrey, which tacks on Chambertin, its most famous vineyard, to become Gevrey-Chambertin. Wine sold as Gevrey-Chambertin comes from areas around the town which do not rate individual vineyard status. Except in unusual circumstances not a drop will be from Le Chambertin. It is crucial that you understand this because the quality difference is significant (see page 129). All of the vineyards here taken together produce an exceptional amount of Burgundy, most of them reliable and good. They share a powerful smoothness and an identifiably dark color.

Le Chambertin, too, has its myths. It was Napoleon's favorite wine. What isn't often mentioned is that he mixed it with water.

At Morey-St.-Denis we have a transition. The first half of the commune is a continuation of the hills of Chambertin and its wines are quite similar. Below the midpoint, however, we hit a new style of tastes. The wines from this and the next series of communes develop an exquisite, feminine style that is the pinnacle of the world's great wines. The towns are famous: Chambolle-Musigny, Vougeot and Vosne-Romanée. One could easily write a chapter on each and many frequently have.

This group of communes adds more finesse and a more delicate nose to the attributes of those of the north. Chambolle-Musigny, the first village after Morey-St.-Denis, still has some of the power, but its wines seem to be warmer, more spread out and mellow. By the time you are in Vougeot (as in Clos Vougeot) the wine is of a lighter color, though no less intense, and will show very refined breed and great finesse.

The name Clos de Vougeot is so famous that it almost eclipses the other great vineyard in its commune, Echezeaux. It would appear that every wine writer is obliged to mention that Echezeaux is a comparative bargain, which it is. They say that this is because Echezeaux is unpronounceable, which it isn't. Just say it as if you were sneezing. That's the way it sounds.

The last commune, Vosne-Romanée, is the ultimate in the great feminine style of wine. Less than a mile wide, it contains at least five of the world's finest vineyards. These include Richebourg, Romanée-St.-Vivant, La Romanée, La Tâche and most renowned of all, Romanée-Conti. They have balance, breed, majesty and intensity, the key to great wine. The production is minimal, the price astronomical, and the occasion rare when any of us has the privilege to try these.

The Côte de Nuits ends in Nuits-St.-Georges. Its wines lack the finesse of its near neighbors. They harken back to those of farther north, but here with a touch less power.

COTE DE BEAUNE

The vineyards recommence after a short break for farmland at Aloxe-Corton. It is the first commune in the Côte de Beaune and, in terms of taste, it stands by itself. If you have seen pictures of Ayer's Rock in Australia, then you know what the hill of Corton looks like, except on a smaller scale. It stands alone on the slightly rolling landscape. The vineyards highest up its slopes are the best—but all are good. It is an odd rule in wine and is probably linked to drainage factors, but *the best wines do tend to come from the middle of the slope.*

The hill of Corton is an extension of the escarpments of the Côte de Nuits, and its wines resemble them in weight and power. On the back side of the hill is a little, relatively unknown town called Pernand-Vergelesses. Its wines are smaller but still distinguished. By being outside the limelight, it tends to be a bargain.

Next comes the grouping of Beaune, Pommard and Volnay. Monthé-lie and Auxey-Duresses may be considered their satellites in much the same relationship that Pernand has to Corton: under-appreciated and the home of potentially good values. All the wines of the Côte de Beaune (all things being equal) share a lightness of body when compared to the Côte de Nuits. The color is often more red than purple, but that varies with the quality of the vintage. The wines are soft, wonderful wines but they lack the concentrated intensity that make some wines unique. As the description implies, they are comparatively quick to mature.

These descriptions seem a bit pat, as if the wines were exactly one thing and you could perfectly define them. They are not. A *négociant* is the man in Burgundy who takes the place of the château owner of Bordeaux. He shapes the wine to his style. He may grow the grapes, or he may buy them. In any case, he vinifies and blends the wine. The final product is his and he places his stamp on the result. A man like Jacques Prieur can make a Beaune as heavy as a Chambertin. The weight may change, and the amount of tannin he induces into the wine may affect its aging potential, but if it is a good wine it will still retain the characteristics of its origins.

We skip the next portion of the Côte de Beaune. It produces incomparable white wines; we will not neglect them long but will return to them in the next section. Beyond this are the two final red-wine towns of consequence: Chassagne-Montrachet and Santenay. The Chassagne-Montrachets of recent memory have been very light red wines almost bordering on being an extremely deep rosé. Their wine is thus rather delicate. To me it is as if their being from vineyards that also produce white wines has affected them. The Santenays have been similarly light, rather fat wines. The warmer sun seems to make them enjoyable, fruity but uncomplex.

As you assess today's Burgundies, look at their color and notice their over-all lightness, you may begin to think that some of the older books have misled you. Where is the overwhelming body, the mystical bouquet, the deep Burgundian color? Gone, most of it is gone. The Pinot Noir grape used today as mentioned earlier is bigger than its pre-World-War-II forebear. It gives more juice but has a lower proportion of skin surface. The skin gives color, tannin and some of the taste. The wine is paler today and will mature faster. There are a few of the old style wines left. *Négociants* like Prieur, Dujal, Jadot, Louis Latour and Faiveley make them, but then you have to be prepared to lay them away and gamble on their coming around. The new style better faces the realities of today.

TASTING 19: Red Burgundies

When one is talking high quality, one is also talking high cost. You cannot escape it, Bungundies are expensive. The ideal tasting would include one representative wine from each of the different taste groups I've mentioned. For most people this is not realistic, so we must pare it down.

It is possible to do it with just one wine. If you know how to locate a perfect Burgundy of a good year and respectable age, you can do it. But I've found Burgundies to be very chancy wines. You have to try quite a few before you find one that you like. A high price helps. So does the name of a good shipper. But neither is a guarantee.

If you do decide to splurge on a single ten- or fifteen-dollar bottle, it should be from one of the best vineyards of the southern Côte de Nuits.

Preferred: Le Musigny
             Clos Vougeot
             Échezeaux (Grand)
             Richebourg
             Romanée-St.-Vivant

La Romanée
La Tâche
La Grande-Rue
Romanée-Conti
Le Chambertin
Chambertin-Clos de Béze

Alternatives: Any Premier Cru vineyard in the communes of the Côte de Nuits or of Corton.

Vintages: 1964 Fine year, but may be getting old except for the finest.

1966 Ditto, but more copious and perhaps lighter.

1967 A very fine year with the better wines at their peak.

1969 Extraordinary year, powerful and long lasting.

1970 A good lighter, delicate year now ready.

1971 Another very fine year; may still be too young.

1972 Very good under-appreciated year; much fruit and power.

1976 A fine year but too young.

Shippers: Heavy style: Jacques Prieur
Medium style: La Marche

Hopefully this wine will show the immense appeal of a Burgundy. It should come out and say "welcome home, I always liked you." The bouquet is like a rare spice perfume. It is intangible and indefinable, but most like fruits and berries. Perhaps it is the texture of the wine that most clearly identifies it as a great Burgundy. It has a tactile smoothness that makes it feel like velvet. It is rich and complex and mouth-filling. The aftertaste lingers and changes.

With one wine you must be alert to recognize its underlying difference from the others. Depending on the wine you've chosen, it may be lighter, heavier, etc. My descriptions will have to be your guide until you try some others and gain perspective.

One wine may give you an idea of quality, but really it is not sufficient. It would be best to compare the Côte de Nuits to the Côte de Beaune. In this case it is not necessary to choose the most expensive wine. Wines typical of the style will do, and you can get that benchmark from most estate-bottled wines. To see the Pinot Noir in its guises try to pick extremes: Contrast a heavy Fixin or Morey-St.-Denis with a Beaune or red Chassagne-Montrachet.

	Côte de Nuits	vs.	*Côte de Beaune*
Preferred:	Morey-St.-Denis		Beaune
	Fixin		Chassagne-Montrachet
Alternatives:	Chambolle-Musigny		Volnay
	Nuits-St.-Georges		Pommard
			Santenay

Optional: Add the best Vosne-Romanée, Clos Vougeot or Chambolle-Musigny you can afford.

Vintages: As in previous tastings, but including:
1973 A prolific and light year.
1975 Good but young.

The wines should pretty well parallel the description in the text. The northern wine should be big, earthy and powerful. The southern, from a more obviously sunny clime.

Consumerism. Buying Burgundies is not like buying Bordeaux. A Château Rausan-Ségla is pretty predictable. You get to know what to expect. Not so in Burgundy. First of all, there is much more reliance on commune wines in Burgundy than there is in the Médoc. You have no knowledge other than the town name as to the precise plot where the wine came from. So now, you not only have to learn the characteristics of the towns, but the reputations of the shippers (*négociants*) as well. As if this weren't enough, you must also expect the shippers to be inconsistent. Their fortunes rise or fall, owners die, firms change hands or sometimes they are just plain erratic. It ends up that the only way to buy Burgundy is to canvass the stores and set up a tasting to see which wines are good. As a general method for selecting a Burgundy, first you pick a vineyard, then you find a shipper. Of the two, the former is more important for the character of the wine and the latter, hopefully, for reliability.

Lastly—in case you are still in any doubt—Burgundy is too expensive for use as your common house wine. There are other areas which are similar in style but which are much less expensive. Probably the best are the excellent wines made from the Nebbiolo grape (also called Spanna) from the Swiss border region of Italy. Enough of these can still be found which are ten to fifteen years old and cost from $4.00 to $7.00. Good Châteauneuf-du-Pape and other Côte-du-Rhône wines have a similar big body and gutsy, earthy style.

As I continuously point out, all charts are faulty, and especially one that tries to come to grips with a winemaker's style. He may change over time, or his style may vary according to whether he owns the vineyard and can control the grapes, or just buys them. Still, an attempt is necessary as a means of conveying information.

The divisions light, medium and heavy refer strictly to the style, and have no bearing on price or quality. A light style can cost more than a heavy one and be a better wine.

BURGUNDIAN WINEMAKERS' STYLES

Light		*Medium*		*Heavy*
Jaboulet			Drouhin	Dujac
Grivelet		Remy		
	Clair-Dau		Prieur	L. Latour
	Bouchard			
			Leroy	
		L'Héritier-Guyot		Rousseau
	Noëllat		Jadot	
Chauvenet			Faiveley	
		La Marche		Trapet
	Jaffelin		Morin	
		Roumier		
	Vienot	Jayer		
	Gros	Villemont	Comte de Vogüë	

WHITE BURGUNDIES

All the serious dry white wines of the world should be thought of as a single group, because they share a kinship which reds do not: They are all (except Champagne) made *exclusively* from the Chardonnay grape. The Sauvignon is also a noble grape, but even in its home, Graves, it does not produce white wine of sufficient complexity and character to rival the great whites of Champagne, Chablis, Montrachet and California. In this chapter, we will also include the Mâcon district by way of rounding out the areas where the Chardonnay is grown. In Mâcon, however, it is prolific, not prestigious.

With so many regions using the same grape, the study of Chardonnay wines becomes an exceptionally revealing exercise. It is a microcosm of everything that can happen to a wine. Its districts are hundreds or perhaps thousands of miles apart. What unites them in greatness should be interesting to discover. It is a matter of climate, geology and vinification methods. Each region has one of these making its maximum impact.

What are the great Chardonnay districts?

Champagne springs most quickly to mind, though because of its uniqueness there may be some argument as to how to classify it. Most Champagne is a blend of Pinot Noir (fermented off the skins so there is no color) and Chardonnay. Some is made predominantly from Chardonnay, and that is labeled Blanc de Blancs.

Next is *Chablis*, whose chalky soil and northern climate make a lean, austere wine.

South of this we hit the *Côte de Beaune* in Burgundy. It is one of the two great white-wine regions of the world. Purists will frown, but California, the upstart region, is making a serious bid to topple Burgundy as king of the mountain. But more of that later.

Below the Côte d'Or we come to the last region, the *Mâcon.* These wines may not be great but they are the next best thing. At $3.00 a bottle or less, we will all drink cases of these for any bottle of the fancier wine. And besides, there is a family resemblance that is worth studying.

These are the wines we will be using so let's take a closer look.

Champagne

Champagne is never taken seriously except when you pay for it. Yet in many ways it is one of the most complex wines you can buy. For one thing, it is obvious that there are more processes involved in making it than there are for other wines. Basically the grapes are crushed and fermented in the usual way to produce wine, except that red grapes are used in most Champagnes, so the juice must be drawn off the skins quickly before pigmentation gives a tint to the wine. Because Champagne is very far north, the grapes tend to have a high acid content. The cool winters allow the juice to ferment very slowly, and low temperatures cause the strong tartaric acid to precipitate out in the form of crystals. By spring, the wine is fully dry and less biting. Next, the wine must be blended; then the sparkle must be induced.

Each of the areas within Champagne produces grapes with a distinct character. Those from the hillsides between Rheims and Epernay would make a wine of superior body. Others from south of Epernay give you more finesse. The ideal is a wine with everything, and that is why Champagne is blended, or as they call it, making a *cuvée*.

Once the *cuvée* has been agreed upon, they bottle the wine and add an additional dose of sugar and some more yeast (the old yeast had died with the ending of the first fermentation). Then they tightly seal the bottle. The sugar is food for the little yeast beasts, so they will start a second fermentation. But this time carbon dioxide, which is the by-product, cannot escape, so it is trapped as carbonization; thus you get Champagne.

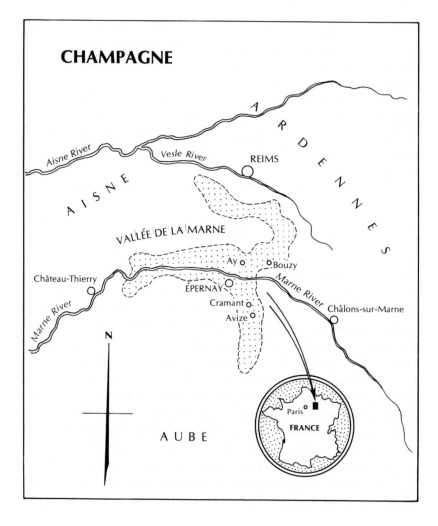

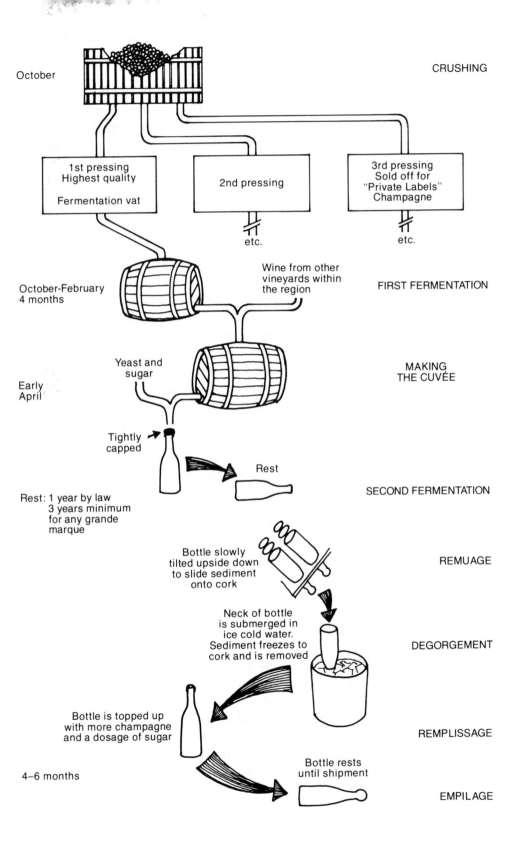

October — CRUSHING

1st pressing
Highest quality

Fermentation vat

2nd pressing

3rd pressing
Sold off for
"Private Labels"
Champagne

etc.

etc.

October–February
4 months — FIRST FERMENTATION

Wine from other
vineyards within
the region

Yeast and
sugar

Early
April — MAKING
THE CUVÉE

Tightly
capped

Rest

Rest: 1 year by law
3 years minimum
for any grande
marque — SECOND FERMENTATION

Bottle slowly
tilted upside down
to slide sediment
onto cork — REMUAGE

Neck of bottle
is submerged in
ice cold water.
Sediment freezes to
cork and is removed — DEGORGEMENT

Bottle is topped up
with more champagne
and a dosage of sugar — REMPLISSAGE

4–6 months

Bottle rests
until shipment

EMPILAGE

There is one final step, however. The adding of the yeast makes an unsightly sediment that must be expelled. Over a period of months, as the Champagne ages (still on the yeast), the bottle is gradually turned neck side down and gently rotated. This moves the sediment onto the cork. The neck is then immersed in ice-cold water which freezes it; when the cork is pulled, the frozen sediment comes away with a minimum loss of wine. That is called disgorging. The bottle is then topped up with old Champagne mixed with sugar cane and perhaps a shot of brandy. That completes the process. The Champagne is now in the same form in which you will buy it.

The relative sweetness or dryness of Champagne is totally controllable. It is a function of the sugar cane added. Starting with the driest, Champagne runs brut, sec, demi-sec, but the trade admits that people "buy dry but drink sweet," meaning that the wines aren't as excessively dry as they claim. A totally "natural" Champagne could be unpalatable.

The French are very fussy about the use of the name Champagne. There was once a law suit in an English court over the right to call any sparkling wine "Champagne." The prosecutor attacked the expert witness, accusing him of wanting to reserve the word "Champagne" only for the most expensive kinds of Champagne so that only the rich could enjoy it. To which Raymond Postgate is supposed to have replied, "What you want to do is call margarine butter, so the poor can enjoy butter." There is Champagne and then there is the rest.

Champagne seems inseparable from anecdotes and I do not know if the following is a true story, but it seems to tell well. You may be curious as to the origins of those shallow fruit cup-type glasses in which waiters still insist on serving Champagne. Apparently they were started by Marie Antoinette, who had four glasses molded in the shape of her breasts. It became a nice tradition if one liked his champagne and his women flat, and is more fashionable than drinking out of a slipper, but hardly something to lose your head over. For enhancing the Champagne and saving on cleaning bills, long-fluted glasses are preferred.

Even sophisticated wine buffs don't seem aware that there are different styles of champagne. Naturally, there is vintage and non-vintage. The non-vintage is a mixture of several years, which has the effect of playing off different ripenesses, acid levels, etc., in order to achieve a uniform product. Vintage Champagnes are more expensive and are only made in exceptional years. But this is not what I meant by different styles. Some Champagnes are made with a higher proportion of

Pinot Noir grapes, and that gives them a fuller body. Some tradition-
alists still ferment in oak. This too adds some character. Some houses
leave the wine on the yeasts up to ten years before disgorging. That
wonderful and expensive habit gives a richness and complexity that
is not easily forgotten. These Champagnes are not suited to be apéritifs.
They are too substantial. These are the ones you have with food. They
have the backbone to stand up to solid fare. Lighter wines, ones made
totally from Chardonnay or having a higher proportion of it are preferred for sipping alone or drinking with the light parts of the meal.
Neither style has a quality advantage over the other, but you'll enjoy
them more if you try each in its place.

In order to be helpful, I have attempted a division of some of the
major brands of Champagnes according to their styles as I see them.

Full and Robust:	Any rosé irrespective of brand
	Krug
	Bollinger
	Veuve Clicquot
	Roederer
	Launois
Mellow:	Ayala
	Mumm
	Moët & Chandon
	Pol Roger
Light and Elegant:	Any Blanc de Blancs
	Taittinger
	Laurent Perrier
	Piper Heidsieck
	Charbaut

In all there are over two hundred Champagne houses. Most are
obscure; a mere dozen dominate the United States market. They sell
Champagne under their own well-known labels, but a few will also sell
to retailers or restaurateurs who will put their own house-brand labels
on the bottle. The way to tell if you are buying an original bottling
or a private label is to look for the small code on the label. If it
shows "N.M." followed by some numbers, then it is from the original
Champagne house. If it says, "M.C." and numbers, then it is a private
brand. A private brand will only be as good as the person you are
buying it from.

The most famous and largest house is Moët & Chandon. It is a huge company run by the Comte de Vogüe, which also owns Christian Dior fashions and Hennessy Cognac as well as other important Burgundian vineyards. Part of the interest of the company to us should be that it also has "Champagne" vineyards in Argentina and one coming on line in our Napa Valley. The Argentinian wine is not available to us, but their Napa sparkling wine may be. They've even sent over some of their best winemakers to start the American venture in a manner in which they can feel comfortable. A comparison of that to the regular French bottling is fascinating. It shows why real Champagne is unique.

TASTING 20: Champagnes

Most of the talk on Champagnes has gotten us away from our real topic, which is the great Chardonnays. Only those marked Blanc de Blancs (using Chardonnay grapes only) can be of use to us. Because they are now in fashion and not because of any intrinsic superiority on their part, Blanc de Blancs seem to require a higher price. I suppose this is another reflection of the general belief that lighter is better. There are a few all-Chardonnay Champagnes that aren't too expensive. One is Charbaut, from an aggressive importer who has made a respected name for himself by under-pricing and thereby outselling his more established and better-known competition.

The Champagne tasting need involve only two bottles, although spirits improve if you have more. To me the archetype of the great traditional Champagne is the Bollinger R.D. The R.D. means "recently disgorged," and was the one I referred to that may have sat on its yeast for up to ten years. Apparently Champagnes will keep almost indefinitely in that condition—twenty years—and always become richer. Surprisingly the R.D. costs only (only?) about $18.00, which is a bargain when measured against the $30.00 prices of some of the other premium têtes de cuvées.

The other would be a representative of the light and elegant style. If you choose a Blanc de Blancs, then you can marry this tasting with the white Burgundy tasting later. If you want an elegant Champagne in the traditional Pinot Noir/Chardonnay blend, then try a Pol Roger. It is an outstanding Champagne but a damn nuisance to locate. Any of the other light-style Champagnes (or Moët) will stand well in the comparison.

	Preferred	*Alternative*
Full:	Bollinger R.D.	Krug
Elegant:	Pol Roger	Taittinger

Consumerism. The occasions for buying Champagne for the home, in a restaurant or for celebration, will increase over the years. A knowledge of how much to spend and what quality you will get in return can save you a lot of money. Since Champagne is the ultimate social wine, it is the aid to special occasions and not the center of them. So, to be candid, I find the best of them can be wasted on me. In such circumstances, who can give them the attention they deserve? If you adjust your pricing to your level of perception, you may find that there are a number of Champagnes or near-Champagnes available for $5.00 to $9.00 that are a perfect pleasure even for the most sophisticated crowd. But when you want quality, then style enters into it. So, learn which houses please you.

Chablis

In many ways color is more important for white wines than for reds. That is because whites age more quickly. A light, healthy color is important for the dry wines. A deep yellow or gold is almost always a sign of age, and indicates that oxidation has taken place. Some young wines are straw colored; some have the slightest aspect of steely grey; but Chablis has a definite green tint which I suspect is tied to its high-acid level.

The sun is not very strong in Chablis. It is as far north in Burgundy as you can get. Not much sugar is produced, so the wines stay tart with that characteristic bite that allows it to cut through the metallic overtones of raw oysters. All the sugar is fermented to provide Chablis its necessary alcohol. The result is a bone-dry wine with a lighter body than some of the southern Burgundies you will later be comparing it with.

The flexibility of the Chardonnay does not protect it from the worst weather. The climate in Chablis can be ruinously cold and there can be bad hail. Hail knocks off the leaves, and the berries will then not ripen. A bad Chablis is a very bad wine. I recall a 1972 Premier Cru that was fobbed off on me in a restaurant in New York. Green mold will form on my American Express card before I pay that wine bill.

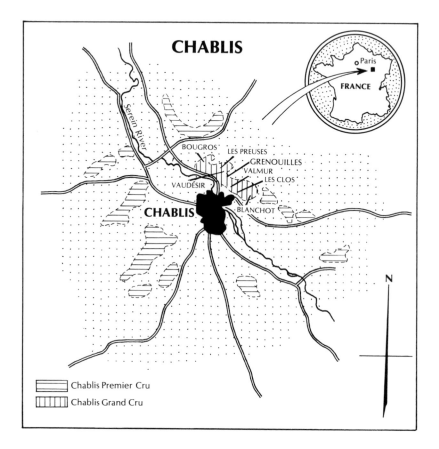

TASTING 21: Chablis

Chablis is organized in a most interesting and understandable way.
The outlying areas are allowed to call themselves Petit Chablis. The
center with better soil is Chablis. Within this are twenty-four* vineyards that rate Premier Cru status. They usually note this on their
labels. The top of the line is the seven Grand Cru plots. Here is another lesson in quality recognition such as we had in Chapter V. Try a
vertical tasting involving a regular Chablis, a Premier Cru and a Grand
Cru. They should all be readily available.

---

* Now consolidated into eleven names.

VIN DE BOURGOGNE

CHABLIS
St Vincent
APPELLATION CHABLIS CONTROLÉE

Caves Chanson (Ancien bastion du XVᵉ Siècle) à Beaune

CHANSON

PRODUCED, BOTTLED AND SHIPPED BY

CHANSON PÈRE & FILS, NÉGOCIANTS-ÉLEVEURS, BEAUNE (COTE-D'OR) FRANCE
12 FL. OZ.   PRODUCE OF FRANCE   ALCOHOL 11,5 % BY VOL.

Château Grenouille Testut
Chablis Grand Cru
APPELLATION CHABLIS GRAND CRU CONTROLÉE

1973

Mise en bouteille
à la propriété
Contents 1 Pint 8 Fl. Oz.

PRODUCT OF FRANCE
White Table Wine
Estate Bottled

M.M.TESTUT FRÈRES
Chablis-89-Yonne
Alcohol 12,5% by volume

SOLE U.S. AGENT

Crosse & Blackwell Vintage Cellars, Inc.

SAN FRANCISCO, CA.   NEW YORK, N.Y.

Preferred:

Chablis:	Determine by availability
Premier Cru:	Most are reputable
Grand Cru:	Most are reputable
Vintages:	See listing page 28, but preferably a good year like 1976.

Consumerism. What I have noticed is that the price break between a rated growth and a regular Chablis is not sufficient to account for the serious increase in quality. In addition, the production of the rated growths is more closely monitored, so you can feel more assured of their authenticity. Many things are called Chablis which were never grown there.

The Côte de Beaune

Most great white wine comes from the southern section of the Côte d'Or, the real heart of Burgundy. The quantity that is made in the Côte de Nuits is so small that it almost amounts to a novelty. There is a high-priced Blanc Clos de Vougeot and also a white Nuits-St.-Georges made from an albino version of the Pinot Noir. They are very useful for confusing friends—it was done to me yesterday—but the serious core of production lies further south, in the Côte de Beaune. There is a little stretch starting at the village of Meursault that, together with a tiny section of the western face of the hill of Corton, are nearly the world's only source of *great* white wine. Their fame exceeds their quantity.

Why do white Burgundies hold this unique position? There are elements to the best of them that no other white wine has. We enjoy most whites in an almost thoughtless way for their youth and freshness. A few, like Chablis, have a crispness and a certain complexity that give them more sophistication. But none are like a great white Burgundy, which will have the best qualities of the best red wines without its drawbacks. White Burgundies can age, and thereby take on subtle flavoring. They have body so they can convey that message. And from the sun, grape, and soil, they have complexity which gives a rich and concentrated flavor. They have the power and bigness of a red wine and the delicacy of a white. That is what they can be—but of late it seems that I have also been tasting a lot of failures.

White Burgundies are organized in roughly the same manner as the reds. There are commune wines, which seek to gain marketing prestige by hyphenating the name of their most famous vineyard onto the town's name. Thus you have Chassagne-Montrachet and Puligny-Montrachet because the great Montrachet vineyard straddles both communes. Then

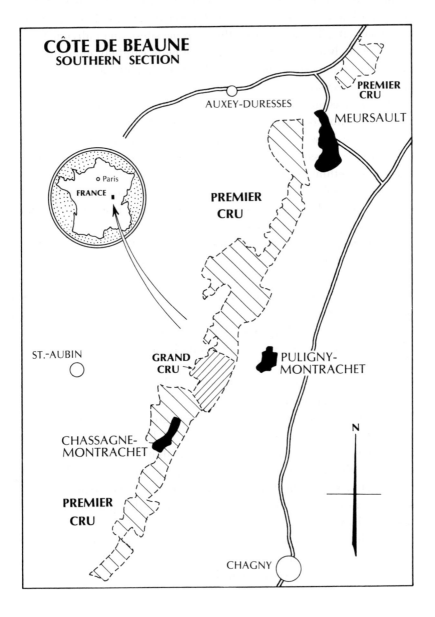

CÔTE DE BEAUNE
SOUTHERN SECTION

AUXEY-DURESSES

PREMIER CRU

MEURSAULT

FRANCE

o Paris

PREMIER CRU

ST.-AUBIN

GRAND CRU

PULIGNY-MONTRACHET

N

CHASSAGNE-MONTRACHET

PREMIER CRU

CHAGNY

there are the individual vineyards. These are divided into Premier Cru and Grand Cru, with the latter receiving the top billing. Any estate-bottled wine, that is one coming from a classified vineyard, should have the potential for greatness.

Like Chablis, the commune wines are vulnerable to impersonation. Shippers have been known to stretch the Puligny-Montrachet label. As always, a known shipper and a good merchant are the best guarantees of authenticity. The wines from the supreme sites—the individual vineyards—will always be genuine. They are more carefully monitored and the pride of important men depends on their authenticity. They are also quite expensive.

The main communes are Meursault, Puligny and Chassagne. Their vineyards follow one after another so neatly that it is hard to say why a distinction between them is valid. Yet it is. If the climate and the exposure are the same, it must be a subsurface change in the soil. There must be something in the light colored marl and in the lime that affects the scent. Chablis gets its freshness from its chalk soil. Montrachet, by contrast, probably gets its body and almond spice from its soil, which is thirty-one percent limestone.

The difference between Le Montrachet and the other Grand Cru vineyards is a matter of nuances in power and delicacy. Between them and the Premier Crus, the difference is a matter of personal reaction. A fine bottle of any of them will render written generalizations meaningless. All of the best of them will have an excellent balance between tartness and restrained ripeness. The bouquet will be quite wonderful. It will most likely hint of wood and vanilla because these wines are aged longer than most in oak. There may also be spice in the best of these wines, and all the good ones should have a long, lingering aftertaste of fruit and cellar memories.

In poor years these wines can taste very green and acidic. Then they won't have grace because they are out of balance. To increase the alcohol level in those vintages when the sun didn't shine, the winemakers chaptalize the wine: They add sugar. If properly done it will save the wine, but never make it very good. From the wines that have been showing up in the United States, I think that this practice has lately been much overused.

The white Burgundy area is too small, the price too high and the differences between them too minor to require a tasting. Instead, at least one representative wine will be used in the total Chardonnay tasting.

ELSEWHERE

There are a number of other areas that use the Chardonnay grape, and this is where we get the bulk of our excellent drinking wines. To put this in perspective: It's nice to know Chevalier Montrachet once a month, but I'll be drinking (Pinot) Chardonnay Mâcon daily. My pride is not in the $30.00 bottles I own but in the fact that I know where to find fine wines for just a few dollars. It is more important to know the small wines than the large.

There are many areas that use the Chardonnay to satisfy the bulk of our thirst. The most popular besides Mâcon is Pouilly-Fuissé. Some of the others would be Mercurey and the wines of the Chalonnais. Lesser wines here may be made from the Aligoté grape and will hopefully be so labeled.

These $2.00 and $3.00 wines form a special category. They involve our consumption needs, not our connoisseur needs. The fancy wines may teach you potential, but the inexpensive ones will teach you value.

California Chardonnay

Why include our West Coast when we are supposed to be examining Burgundy? It is because these two areas are beginning to be recognized as rivals, and as always rivals have much in common. All up and down the quality scale California wines are a reasonable alternative and in some arenas even beat the pants off the French in price effectiveness. The Côte d'Or wines have cachet but the West Coast whites may be an idea whose time has come.

It would be lovely to be able to tell you in three or four sentences the themes that make California wines understandable, but they don't exist. The geographic differences that we use elsewhere do not apply here. The state breaks down into so many micro-climates that it is possible to grow grapes in valleys south of Los Angeles that are cooler than those north of San Francisco. If there is any key, it is this concentration on temperature (see heat summation, page 63). Grapes develop best within certain ranges. Some are cool and some require protracted warmth. Unfortunately we do not find very much information about this on the labels of any but the most expensive wines.

There are other factors which we will discuss in detail in the next chapter. Some people, for instance, speak of the superiority of grapes grown on the steep hillsides over those from the valley floor, but that is probably due as much to the increased care and decreased yields as anything else.

Napa Valley is the area that has gained the most prestige for its premium Chardonnay, so it is best to start with the wineries from here and the neighboring Sonoma. In a comparison for value with the French, pair wines of each price range. At $3.00 I haven't found much worth while in California, so the Mâcon prevails. However, starting at $5.00, the Coast wines get exciting. At $5.00 see how one stands up to a Chablis. The result will depend as much on which California vineyard you select as on your own preference as to style.

At the $7.00 range we begin to see an interesting division. Two styles emerge in California, one is light and delicate, with noteworthy finesse. Such would be a Chardonnay from Robert Mondavi. Then there is the other: a unique American evolution. These are unusually heavy wines, frequently one or two percent higher in alcohol than the average and hence having more body. Their character is nearly overwhelming, and there is most often a strong taste of oak. They are most interesting and intriguing wines. The standard-bearer for this style is David Bruce.* Others include Spring Mountain, Chalone, and Château Montelena. Wines of this peerage should only be compared to Burgundian heavyweights like Chevalier Montrachet, Bienvenue-Bâtard-Montrachet, or even to that section of Le Montrachet itself that is owned by Marquis de Laguiche (whose wines have been underwhelming lately).

TASTING 22: Great Dry White Wines

With such a panoply of choices, what wines would be best for the tasting? Certainly Champagne is optional, although it would be a wonderful gesture for the more well-heeled amongst us. Chablis, definitely yes. You face it everywhere: From fine wine lists to concocted Spanish wine labels. It is the standard for all dry white wine so you should know what the real article tastes like.

A Côte de Beaune wine must be included. Any of the three commune wines will do, or, if you are more ambitious, one of the fine

---

* At fifteen and one-half percent alcohol his 1973 Late Harvest Chardonnay is almost too powerful to be classed as a wine. It is inspiring, immense, with the gripping appeal of an *auslese* but overlaid with Chardonnay's green acidity, firm body and austere complexity.

estate-bottled wines listed below would be fine. There is a logic for a bit of extravagance. In the world's eyes, the various Montrachet wines and Corton Charlemagne are the ultimates. If the Californias are coming on hard, you should know what they are being judged against. You should pay special attention to your own feelings as to whether you feel you are receiving sufficient additional quality for the higher price you pay.

Any of the other Chardonnay wines (Mâcon, Pouilly-Fuissé, etc.) which experience has taught you to enjoy should also be included.

California wines should definitely be included for all the reasons we've already mentioned. If you are tasting four price categories of French wines, then match them with the best equivalently-priced American wines you can find. You may want to pre-read the chapter on California Chardonnays first. As a final option, you may want to consider a California "Chablis." It could be illuminating.

Preferred:

1. Any Grand or Premier Cru Chablis from any shipper 1971, 1973, 1975, 1976.

2a. A Meursault, Chassagne-Montrachet or Puligny-Montrachet 1971, 1973, 1976 bottled by Bouchard, Père, Drouhin, Gros, Jaboulet, Jadot, Latour, Prieur, Remy, Ropiteau, Sichel, Thevenin or Thorin. This list is not exclusive so other good shippers will do but a good shipper is as meaningful as where the wine claims to be from.

2b. and/or, An estate-bottled wine from any of the Premier or Grand Cru vineyards of Corton, Puligny or Chassagne.

3. Any chardonnay from Mâcon, the Chalonais, Pouilly-Fuissé or other similar area that you would consider suitable for your everyday wine.

4. At least one California wine from whichever price category you prefer:

under $5	*over $5*
Sonoma 1974 or later	Joseph Phelps
Wente	Robert Mondavi
	David Bruce

Consumerism. The tasting itself should show a lot about value in white wines. It has been my experience that under $3.00, nothing can touch the Mâcons, and at around $5.00 the genuine French Chablis is best—although some of the California Chardonnays show extremely well starting at that price. To me, above $7.00, I almost always buy California. Many people will not agree, but my experience has been that the grand wines of the Côte de Beaune that reach our shores have been over-priced and more often than not are disappointing as well.

GERMAN WINES

Of all the bottles that have gone into my cellar full and come out empty, the Germans may be my favorites. The words "appealing" and "charming" are at home with these wines. It is probably because the wines here are lighter than any others. They are only nine to eleven percent alcohol, versus eleven to fourteen percent anywhere else in the world. This means that you can sit down and easily enjoy a bottle of Moselle or Rhine all by yourself, something you would never do with a French wine. It is so mild a wine that you could drown in it before you become drunk.

Even fine red wines are fatiguing, and after even a short period your taste buds get saturated. That is why you place them with food; the contrast refreshes. Wines like Beaujolais, which one can drink unaccompanied, are really just simple beverages. Rieslings are, by contrast, incredibly complex and refreshing. What I am referring to of course are not the pleasant wines of commerce (such as Liebfraumilch, Zeller Schwartz Katz, Moselblümchen, etc.) but the estate-bottled wines whose prices may frequently be at the same level but whose interest is infinitely superior.

Whereas France has dozens of important wine-growing regions and a dozen important varieties of grapes, Germany has basically only one major grape and only eleven areas. The grape is the Riesling, and only two areas are pre-eminent: the Moselle-Saar-Ruwer and the Rheingau.

In each area we have studied, we have tried to understand why the wines behave the way they do. In Bordeaux we kept coming back to soil drainage and a north-south continuum. In Burgundy, it was the composition of the soil (limestone, chalk, etc.) compounded by the climatic conditions of the specific regions we were observing. In Germany it's heliocentric: Almost everything centers around the sun and weather.

It is always pointed out that these regions are located preposterously far north, almost on the same latitude as the Great Hudson Bay in Canada. The climate, however, is more moderate, but the sun is still weak and it is the sun that ripens and vitalizes the product of the vines. A poor summer, too much rain or clouds . . . and what you get is fit only for the blending vats.

All the major German wine regions are narrow valleys flooded by rivers. In places, especially on the southern Moselle, the cliffs tower

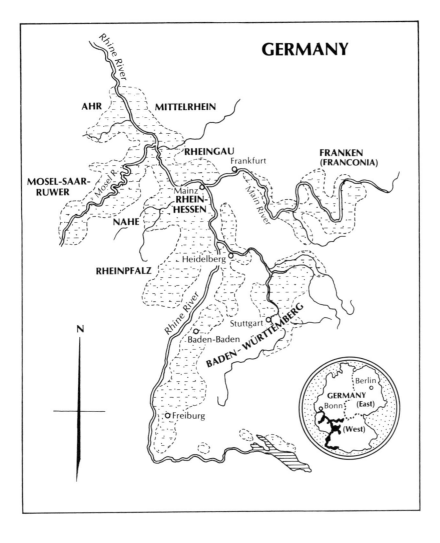

seventy-five stories tall and the steep vineyards are cut like stairs which start at the top and continue to the water's edge. In such conditions machines are of no use, and even such laborious tasks as carrying soil back up after a shower must be done by hand. There is compensation, however. These high hills protect the land from the wind. The river provides a constant warm moisture, and the resulting morning fogs guard against ruinous frosts. The climates of these basins are continental, so the summers are slow and warm without being intense. The growing season is uncommonly long, often continuing into November; in this extra two-month period the vines have the opportunity to absorb a relatively large amount of minerals and other nutrients from the soil, which are responsible for the complex bouquet and aromatic components of the slow-maturing Riesling.

The mountains' protection and the rivers' pampering are necessary compensation for the arbitrariness of this northern climate. There is a vitality that comes to plant and man when they exist at the extremes of nature. The state of stress gives them character. Wines from the warm plains show their indolence by being alcoholic, rich and flabby. By contrast, the Rieslings' constant struggle for existence in the Moselle and Rhine valleys can yield a wine of elegant acidity, voluminous bouquet and ripe fruit sweetness.

The fact that these wines are sweet has led to much misunderstanding. Nowhere has the American wine industry done us a greater injustice than by catering to our Gerber tastes and teaching us to associate sweet wines with cloying, sticky feelings and bad headaches. The German wines plus those of Tokay and Sauternes stand worlds apart from these American confections. Theirs is a natural residual sweetness from the ripe fruit. As in many foods, a touch of sweetness increases the perception of aromatic and taste components of the wine. The sweetness is more rich than it is sweet, and not the least akin to our vapid domestic sugar-added wines.

The German wine regions are narrow valleys that wander in a serpentine fashion. Where they hit a wall of hard stone they turn aside until an easier passage is found. Each new turn is subject to different sun declinations, wind directions and the entire range of environmental variables, including soils. The net effect is that even more than in California each area here has its own micro-climate, its own unique wine taste. There is probably no region of the world better suited for the observation of *goût de terroir*—the changing influence of the soil and climate—than these German wines.

GERMAN WINE LABEL LANGUAGE

Areas:

Regions:

Moselle-Saar-Ruwer:	The Moselle and its tributaries
Rheingau	The heart of great Rhine wines
Rheinhesse	Prolific wine-producing area
Rheinpfalz	Prolific wine-producing area
Ahr	Red wines, seldom seen here
Mittelrhein	Prolific, hearty wines
Nahe	Northern, full-flavored wines
Franken	On the river Main, robust and dry
Baden	Strong reds and whites seldom seen here

Area Sizes:

Gebiet	A region (such as the Rheingau)
Bereich	A district smaller than a region
Grosslage	A collection of contiguous vineyards
Einzellage	A specific vineyard

Quality Terms:

Tafelwein	Standard table wine—for domestic use, seldom a good value when exported
Qualitätswein	Superior quality drinking wine
Qualitätswein mit Prädikat (QmP)	Highest quality wines. All spätlese, auslese, beerenauslese and trockenbeerenauslese must be QmP

Within QmP you have:

Kabinett	The (high) standard grade, light and dryish
Spätlese	Late-picked ripe grapes, richer
Auslese	Specially selected grapes riper still
Beerenauslese	Made from rich clusters attacked by the "noble rot"
TBA	Made from individually selected shriveled grapes attacked by "noble rot"
Eiswein	Rare wine from grapes harvested and crushed frozen; can be any quality level up to TBA

Label Language:

Erzeuger Abfüllung	Estate bottled
Weinkellerei	Wine Cellar (of __)
A.P.Nr.	The wine's official test number, given by the state

Grape types:

Riesling	Müller-Thurgau	Spätburgunder
Sylvaner	Gewürztraminer	

Moselle-Saar-Ruwer

Vineyards line the escarpments of the Moselle as it flows out of France on its way to feed the Rhine. The river snakes back and forth as if it had drunk too much of its own wines. Fifteen miles as the crow flies can take forty of river meandering. The Moselle is important for shipping, and was dredged and widened in 1964. This raised the valley temperature a full two degrees. The widening increased the sunlight reflected onto the vineyards which slant at a steep sixty-degree angle down to the water. The Moselle has two short tributaries, the Saar and the Ruwer. They share enough characteristics that the three are classed as one region. They flow together like a wobbly pitchfork with its handle pointing north.

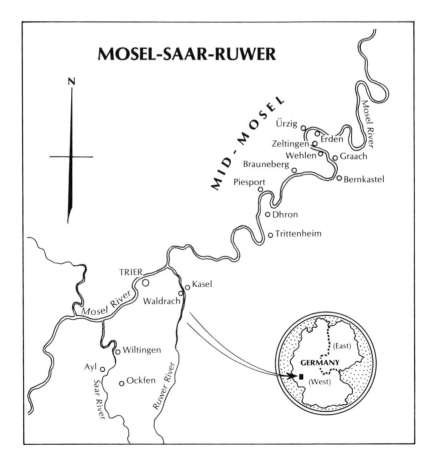

The vineyards are not uniformly distributed. Each of the rivers has its most prolific parts. Only a few towns on the *Saar* are meaningful to us: Ockfen, Ayl and Wiltingen will do for an introduction. On labels "er" is added, Ayl*er* means from the town of Ayl.

Saar wines have the taste of its slate soil. They are hard, steely wines likened in their austerity to Chablis. A fine year makes them among the most desirable in Germany. They also have a richness and fruity depth matched by a crisp stony firmness. The poorer years are not (or should not be) marketed and are usually sold off.

The total vineyard area of the *Ruwer* is so small that it could be passed over if it wasn't that in fine years its three important towns (Eitelsbach, Kasel and Waldrach) make exceptional wine. In those good vintages the wines are as flamboyant as the label of a Maximin Grunhaus. They are spicy, full of flavor and bouquet, but still delicate.

The fine vineyards do not follow one after another. They take a vacation on the Moselle after the Ruwer joins it and do not start up again until Trittenheim. This starts the *Middle Moselle*, the heartland of these wines. Here the vines are planted only on sites facing south, southeast or southwest, in order to catch the maximum sunlight. The ground is a deep grey-blue shale mixed with soft Devonian clay. It captures the day's heat but lets the rains pass through. It is soil which could be used for no other crop. It is tedious to maintain but yields wines of fine pastoral bouquet, steely and pronounced acidity and a delicate prickling flavor.

These wines have breed. Breed seems to be the marriage of the right vine planted in the perfect soil for many, many years. While it might seem odd, this is a taste that comes through in the wine. Breed mirrors aristocracy and to complete the simile, it only occurs on "noble" sites.

Unlike the Saar and Ruwer, every town on the thirty-six miles of the middle Moselle produces wines of character. Each has its individuality. To mention them all and to chronicle each vineyard is unrewarding work, because its production is usually so small that its availability outside Germany is pure caprice. A few of the best that you could be expected to find and, in finding be well rewarded, are wines from:

Trittenheim (er)	Graach (er)
Dhron	Wehlen
Piesport	Zeltingen
Brauneberg	Urzig
Bernkastel	Erden

These are the town names. Individual vineyards would add their names after that of the town such as Trittenheimer Apotheke or Bernkasteler Doktor. As in Burgundy, individual vineyards are often owned by several people. Some of these owners are large firms which have extensive holdings in a whole range of adjacent vineyards. This can make for some interesting comparisons. J. J. Prum, for instance, owns tracts in Bernkastel, in Graacher Himmelreich and in Wehlener Sonnenuhr, all of which are contiguous. Trying one against another shows you how the area changes. Other members of the same family also own land here, and you could match a Wehlener Sonnenuhr from Joh. Jos. Prum against one from Peter Prum. It's the same land, just two different men's styles.

Analogies to the Burgundian system cannot be carried too far. Germany has an entirely different method for classifying its wines from the French. In France, the vineyard is the guarantee of quality. They are classed Grand Cru, Premier Cru, etc.; the top rating is supposed to be the best wine. It is the land that is classified, not the wine. In the eyes of the law, all forty wines from the Clos de Vougeot are judged to be identical.

In Germany, the assumption is different. Here they feel that theoretically any vineyard has the potential to make great wine, so no one site is rated any higher than any other. There is no Grand Cru Classe. Instead, each bottle is judged on its own merits. Government panels do a blind tasting of each wine submitted and rate it. Points are given for clarity (from zero to two), for color (zero to two), for bouquet (zero to four) and for flavor (zero to twelve). The total is then combined with other criteria such as natural sugar content (must weight or öchsle) and for the amound of edelfäule (noble rot). The result is an official government rating. The minimum requirements are:

Quality wines (quality table wines):	11 points
Qualitätswein *mit Prädikat*:	
Kabinett	13
Spätlese	14
Auslese	15
Beerenauslese (BA)	16
Trockenbeerenauslese (TBA)	17

In other words, German law actually guarantees the quality of the wines you are buying. It's entirely possible that in one year a vineyard could produce all its wine *spätlese* or better, and in the following unsuccessful vintage none would even be classed *qualitätswein*. Don't misunderstand this guarantee. It does not say that all spätleses will be of the same quality, but they will at least hold more in common than will a parallel assortment of French Grand Crus.

TASTING 23: The Moselle-Saar-Ruwer

The reason that the same grapes will produce progressively higher qualifications is that each grower may run through his vineyards several times in a successful year and harvest only those grapes that are ripest or at harvesting at least will separate the bunches. The same vineyard and the same man frequently produce a little of each of the above categories in a good year. Since he uses only one distributor to market all his wines, it is quite possible for you to find his *kabinett*, *spätlese* and *auslese* all side by side in the same store. Even a comparison of two is worthwhile and will teach you loads about ripeness. To try three is a treat but if you add a *beerenauslese* or a *TBA*, which are masterpieces, the event will be outstanding.

At the first tasting I would suggest the comparison of the *kabinett* and a higher quality wine. If they are available, all the selections can be from the identical vineyard, but that is not essential. Similar characteristics will be present in any wines labeled *spätlese*, *auslese*, etc., if they are from the same area. Try to be sure they are from the same vintage: 1975 and '76 would be best but 1973, '72 and '71 (the latter a fine year) will do. Let availability govern your choice, but towns of the middle Moselle would be the ones most representative of the area.

In judging them, first note the color. The *kabinett* will be lightest, almost a silver white with a touch of green (a sign of acidity). Each wine up the list will have a deeper, denser golden color. The *TBA* will almost be like a liquor; thick, viscous and deep of color. Age will decrease this distinction moving all toward gold and brown.

The bouquets will be exceptional. There is no mistaking them for any other grape. They are very pronounced and heady, smelling of flowers fruit and honey. But, since they are low in alcohol, your impressions of them will be laced with a delicacy that is unique.

The taste will confirm the nose but will bring out the interplay of acid and richness. If either dominates, the wine is unpleasant; cloying like sugarwater if too sweet; sour and biting if too acid; a joy if balanced. The taste fills the mouth and hints at the *goût de terroir*. The aftertaste lingers, frequently for minutes.

Preferred: Wehlener Sonnenuhr *kabinett* vs. *auslese*
            Graacher Himmelreich *kabinett* vs. *auslese*

Alternatives: Any mid-Moselle estate-bottled wine

Optional: Any Saar or Ruwer estate-bottled wine; any BA or TBA wine preferably from the same year and vineyard.

Bottler: Prum or any reputable name.

Vintage: 1975 or 1976 are preferred but any other good year will do. For some recommendations look at the chart below.

Another tasting would include two or more years from the mid-Moselle. That would show the benefits of aging even a white wine. The same vineyard would be nice, but is not essential just so long as you select wines of equal quality and equal sweetness. Two or three *Cabinet* (using "c" is also done) or *spätlese* would be best, because above that the wines become too individualistic.

Preferred: Same as the above

Bottlers: Same as the above

Vintage: Any combination of these or older years at least three years apart:

> 1971: Great and balanced and picking up complexity from age, but still powerful and far from its peak.
> 1972: A weak year; by comparison to 1971 austere and acid, but shows much finesse.
> 1973: An overly prolific vintage; good drinking wines but thin and lacking intensity.
> 1975: Good, perhaps fine balanced wines; a large crop that year but high quality.
> 1976: Just released but by reputation potentially fabulous— if there is enough acid to balance the almost record-setting ripeness.

A comparison of vineyards within the middle Moselle will teach you only about those sites and not about any continuity among them. This is because the land and exposure change continually as the river bends. You may encounter conditions that have more in common with areas several miles apart than with those of neighbors. Of more use would be an extension of the comparison of the mid-Moselle to the Saar or Ruwer as suggested in the first tasting. The result should show the tributary wines to be harder and more steely, while the Moselles are warmer and more generous.

Consumerism. One of the myths of white wines is that they should all be consumed young. Wrong. It may be true of inexpensive whites, which owe their joyful appeal to youth, but as an assailable generalization *any white over $4.00 should be five years old*. For each $2.00 up to $10.00, add a year of aging. In the sweet French or Germans this is even more true. A simple *kabinett* will improve significantly for five or more years. A *spätlese* for perhaps seven to ten. An *auslese* even more, and the top two, from twenty-five years to half a century. To drink any of them young may be a joy but to let them age is even better.

Now, the trouble with rules like this, and the trouble with vintage charts and all other types of advice is that they require so many modifications, amplifications and exceptions that they make you wish you had never begun. The wines of the Moselle-Saar-Ruwer are lighter than those of the Rhine. They will take a year or two less to reach their peak and will not hold it as long. Also, of course, I assume a fine vineyard and a substantial year.

The Rheingau

If the Moselle is the queen of German wines, the Rheingau is the king. Its wines are powerful, masculine, spicy and elegant. The minute you taste them you know that these are important wines. The Rheingau's success stems from many of the same geographic features that favor the Moselle. It is a deeply carved river valley whose waters act as a mirror for the daylight and as a moderator against sudden chills in early spring and late fall.

The Rhine, which normally flows north at one point, bends ninety degrees to flow east-west for twenty miles. This places the slopes of the protecting Taunus Hills in an ideal position to catch the sunlight from the south. The mist that comes off the river in the mornings protects the vines which grow on the slopes from cold snaps and encourages the growth of edelfäule fungus—the noble rot. This unsightly rot is the same one which works its strange magic in the French Sauternes and also in the Moselle. It punctures the skins of the ripe grapes. The water, which is tasteless, evaporates. The result is a voluptuous concentration of everything that is good. This is how the great *beerenauslese* and *trockenbeerenauslese* are made.

There are a dozen villages along the Rheingau, and if you fall under the spell of the Riesling, their names will soon mean as much to you as Pauillac does to a Bordelaise. But memorizing is tedious work, so let their names become familiar to you by trying them over a period of years. For now, the village need only be a conveniently placed list:

Hochheim (er)	Hallgarten (er)
Eltville	Oestrich
Rauenthal	Winkel—including Schloss Vollrads
Erbach	Johannisberg—including S. Johannisberg
Kiedrich	Geisenheim
Hattenheim—including	Rudesheim
Steinberg	

Again it is hard to generalize about these wines. Many of them command lofty prices, especially in the higher quality gradings. You are

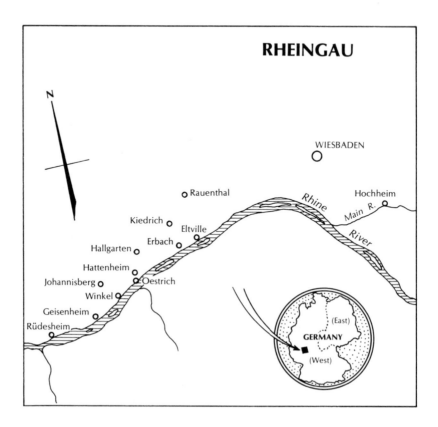

paying for cachet, yes, but also for an individuality of style that is unique to each vineyard, which makes these amongst the noblest and most elegant of all wines. They are the personification of breed, finesse and balance. While they are light of body, they have a firmness and strength of character. Some call it their Prussian backbone. They are *yang* to the Moselle's *ying*.

Because all of the sites have similar sun and climatic exposure, it is the difference in the soil that accounts for a great deal of the vineyard's individuality. The first in the west is Hochheim, which is actually isolated off the mainstream of the Main River. It is on sandy loam. This makes for vigorous soil, which may not be best for the vines. The soil retains more water and the grapes are jucier and less elegant. Still, it does make exquisite wines which were much appreciated by Queen Victoria (and me). In fact it was the Regent's favorite "hock" (English slang for all German wine—a contraction of Hochheimer) and a prominant local owner renamed his vineyard after her: Hochheimer Königin Victoria Berg.

The important string of estates starts at Eltville. From there to Winkel the soil is gravelly, with a base of loam clay and loess. While I am sure that the composition of the soil by no means makes fascinating reading, it does influence the wine. The eastern wines tend to be more powerfully scented and spicy. As you move westward toward Johannisberg, a more delicate perfuminess sets in. The change is fitful, not continuous. Estates downstream can share attributes with some from up river. You must taste your way through the Rhine to get to know them.

TASTING 24: The Rheingau

It is most obvious to match a Rhine with a Moselle to see which appeals to you most. Both should be of the same vintage, quality level (*kabinett* or *spätlese*) and estate bottled. Pairing a 1973 with a 1975 would be misleading.

The first thing you will notice is that the color of the Rheingau will be appreciably deeper. It should be denser with more gold and yellow; the Moselle will be white with a green edge. The bottles they come in seem to recognize this fact. The Rhine bottle is always brown (hence a trademark easy to identify) and the wines within it deep and sturdy. The Moselle has the same distinctive attenuated shape but is always green. Its wine is characteristically sprightly.

When you taste the wines, expect the Rhine to taste less ready. It is slower to mature. There will be some spice to it, perhaps it is a more exotic type of wine. It will show a greater austerity; that masculinity that flows from the gravel soil. The Rhine will have dignity, the Moselle will have wit. Both will fill the mouth and linger a long time with a complexity that beggars description.

While we are comparing regions, you might consider inserting wines from other areas of Germany which we haven't investigated. Here the Riesling grape does not dominate. On the label it might say:

Müller-Thurgau. A grape which is now believed to have been a cross of two Riesling clones but which has its own separate identity. It is light and mild, with a good flower and fruit nose.

Silvaner. It is agreeable and delicate, but a bit too mild.

Spätburgunder. Actually a rosé made from the Pinot Noir grape. It is usually uninteresting but occasionally reverses that, and in rare instances produces a wine with the depth of a Burgundy and the delicacy of a German.

There are other white wine grapes but they don't count for much.

Preferred:	Moselle:	Wehlener Sonnenuhr
		Graacher Himmelreich
		Bernkasteler Graben
	Rheingau:	Erbacher Markobrunn
		Rauenthaler Baiken
		Rudesheimer Rottland
Alternatives:		Any estate-bottled wines from the towns of the Middle Moselle and of the Rheingau.
Optional:		Any of the other nine German wine-producing regions, and their wines can be made from the Riesling or any other grape about which you are curious.
Vintages:		See page 28 for vintage comments
Quality:		*kabinett* or *spätlese*

It is also logical to try the wines within the region. I have already suggested that the wines soften as the Rhine marches west. See if you observe the same tendency. Place a Rauenthaler, an Eltviller or an Erbacher beside a Rudesheimer. See what they share. See how they contrast.

Preferred: Western Rhein: Rudesheimer—any vineyard
           Eastern Rhein: Rauenthaler—any vineyard
                         Eltviller
                         Erbacher

Alternatives: Any combination which (consult the map of the region) would seem as if it would offer an interesting contrast.

Vintages: Wines should be at least three and preferably five years old. See chart on page 28 for comments.

Quality: *kabinett* or *spätlese*

There is one other logical tasting, one that is, along with "Bordeaux versus Burgundy," a classic: Sauternes, the French heavyweight, versus Trockenbeerenauslese, the dessert king. The contest is as unresolvable as it is unfinanceable. It turns out to be a matter of preference, and if friends take opposite sides, the matter will go on all night.

I don't think that it is necessary to go into a long discussion of Sauternes and its relative Barsac; this is not an encyclopedia. I don't mean this as a slight on either. Their delicious sweet wines are among the finest and they can be great bargains. But now that we have practiced the methodology of simple comparison tastings, it is a region you can teach yourself.

For background simply remember that Sauternes and Barsac are part of Bordeaux. Sauternes is more famous and prestigious than Barsac, but once below Château d'Yquem and Chateau Climens many of the estates are on a par. The grape here is the Semillon, not the Riesling as in German wines. It is always blended with Sauvignon Blanc, which adds alcohol and its own unique aroma. The Semillon is a grape of great refinement, bouquet and body. It is a more substantial wine than the Germans, and because of soil and climatic uniformities, Sauternes tend to be more consistent with one another while the Germans tend to be more surprising.

The process is the same as in Germany. The grape is attacked by the "noble rot" and produces a wine of luscious richness. The wine here is fermented to a higher alcohol level than a *trockenbeerenauslese*. The result is a heavier body with more bite. Which has more taste? Well, that's where the argument starts, doesn't it?

Preferred: France: Château d'Yquem
           Germany: Steinberg *Beerenauslese*

Alternatives: The preferred wines are pure fantasy, the Steinberg *BA* could easily cost $100. Other TBA and *beerenausleses* can be found starting at $8.00, but most likely centering around $18.00. Any will do to give you an idea of the rich intensity of these wines. Any château-bottled wine from Sauternes or Barsac will also do, providing it is from a year that was attacked by the rot. Otherwise it will be dry and out of character.

Vintages: At least five years old. See previous charts for vintage evaluations.

Consumerism. For those who prefer dry wines, "off years" like 1972 and 1974 produce the types of wines with which at $2.00 to $3.00 I stock my cellar. They are pleasant, distinctive and dry with some elegance. They may not be great but they are definitely pleasing. I lay them beside my supplies of Mâcon Chardonnay, Loire wines, Rioja and the few cases of inexpensive Californias.

For those times when you want a rich, attention-getting wine like the *TBA* or *beerenauslese*, think in terms of half bottles. These wines are so rich that six or seven people need no more than that. They are like nectar, too intense for straight drinking, perfect for sipping. Also consider Sauternes and Barsac. They are not fashionable right now and their wines are undervalued. From a good merchant, you can occasionally get an amazingly interesting bottle for under $4.00.

In the Rheingau, there are no secrets to finding bargains. The wines are too well known and sought after, especially the select berry pickings. The *kabinetts* and *spätlese* at $3.00 to $5.00 represent good value in excellent wines. My best suggestion is to get a group of friends together when new vintages arrive and try some to decide which is the most appealing choice. Then lay them away for a while.

For any imported German wine, stick with the *Qualitätswein* or the even better *QmP* and avoid any labels reading merely *Tafelwein*.

VII

CALIFORNIA:
THE YOUNG
TRADITION

Not long ago it was easy to identify California wines. They were
light. They had no aging power. They had a uniformity of taste,
a characteristic smoothness as if they had all come from huge vats in
a rationalized production process. There was also an artificial straw-
berry taste (in whites as well as reds) that was a dead giveaway.
Sebastiani's Barbera had it; Beaulieu's Champagne had it.

Now something has happened. It is not that California has stopped
making that type of wine—they still do—but superimposed above this
is a whole new line of craftsmanship, still young and frequently faulty,
whose energy and curiosity is contagious and whose successes are
amazing.

Everyone knew that America could make good bulk table wines,
probably the best in the world. They knew too that some middle-sized
firms in the 1950s and '60s (Krug, Sebastiani, Martini, Wente) made
wines of some individuality that aspired to low premium status. But
now, incubated by the wine boom, has come a new wave of boutique
wineries with talent and ambition. They are a nightmare to study. They
are small and appear and disappear from store shelves with the alacrity
of the Cheshire Cat. They are the subject of cabals. Write one word
of approbation about any of them and the few bottles available vanish.
It's a frustrating business.

California wines are difficult to study because they are organized

like a business and not just like a product of historic evolution. Look
at the semantics. In California you have a winery; anywhere else you
deal with a vineyard. A winery is a production line. It makes red and
white wines: Rieslings alongside Barberas; Chenin Blancs alongside
Zinfandel; Chardonnay alongside Cabernet Sauvignon.

Not all wines will be equally successful. A winery may grow some
of its grapes and buy others. One of the most famous wine makers in
California, Charles Heitz, grows nothing at all. He, like others, buys
on long-term contracts from independents. In the same bottle you may
find juice from both Napa and Sonoma counties. If it's all from Napa,
where in the valley did it come from: The cool south or the warm
north? We know it makes a difference.

The *appellation contrôlée* laws of the civilized wine world have grown
up because certain areas have become recognized for their ability to
make specific consistent and distinctive wines. California has no such
history. If one were to start by trying to isolate a single region that
makes premium wines, one would logically think of Napa first, but
who is prepared to say that the Napa name will mean as much on a
Zinfandel as it does on a Cabernet? As a name, neither Napa nor any
other region is a guarantee of quality.

Price is no guide either. A $6.00 Cabernet is often the match or
even superior to an $8.00 or $10.00 competitor. Expenses in small
wineries are higher per bottle, but small wineries are chic . . . so they
ask and command a premium for rarity which is not necessarily the
same as quality. The most brilliant wines each year are made by these
boutique wineries, but price will not tell you which is which.

Finally we come to the producers. Even they are inconsistent. One
can be quite impressed with Beaulieu for its long run of Cabernets.
Its Private Reserve justly has one of the best reputations in the state,
but its Pinot Noir, to pick on that grape again, is of a much lower
caliber.

The problem is obviously very complex. Even now the government
is struggling to revamp our loose labeling laws—and wishes it weren't
involved. The BATF (Bureau of Alcohol, Tobacco and Firearms), the
normal suzerain, washed its feet of the problem of defining areas (what
should legally be called Sonoma, for example) as too complex and
threw it back to the state to handle. If the big institutions have problems organizing this, how are we to handle it?

Actually what we do is use a bit of everything: The grape type, the
winery's reputation, the vintage year and the location.

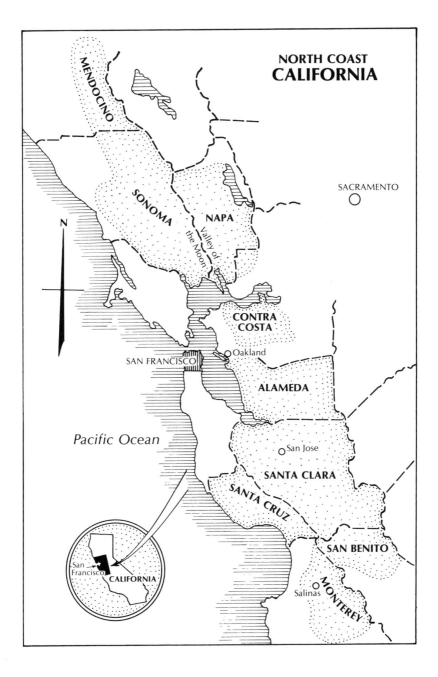

NORTH COAST
CALIFORNIA

MENDOCINO

SONOMA

NAPA

Valley of the Moon

SACRAMENTO

CONTRA COSTA

Oakland

SAN FRANCISCO

ALAMEDA

Pacific Ocean

San Jose

SANTA CLARA

SANTA CRUZ

SAN BENITO

San Francisco

CALIFORNIA

MONTEREY

Salinas

N

Location: That brings up a terribly loaded problem. France has its own "indigenous" grapes. Germany does too. But California has imported all of its vine stock. Its grapes, from Chardonnay to Zinfandel, all are of European origin. Comparisons with Europe become inevitable. Who makes the better Cabernet? How do the Chardonnays compare? And so forth. The answer comes down to what is probably today's most basic and heated argument in wine: perspective.

In California, native wine is part of your lifestyle and it becomes your standard. Its ubiquitousness and price make alternatives an occasional curiosity. You are 7,000 miles from the other nearest serious wine region. You are isolated, and because you have pride in what your state has accomplished, you are also a bit of a chauvinist. I have an East Coast palate, which probably means that my standards are more European. The difference is subtle, but it most likely means that a Californian compares all wines to the Californias, while an Easterner compares them to the French. It has led to obvious disagreements on wines between Eastern and Western tasters. I have been a slow convert —but a convert I am. Californians appreciate their wines so much because they don't have other standards for comparison. If I were weaned on Wente Grey Riesling without knowledge of its German namesake I would probably like it more than I do. Having admitted this prejudice, or rather perspective, I can praise those California wines that are good and criticize those that fall short. There should be no special rules here. What is excellent is what can compete on an international scale.

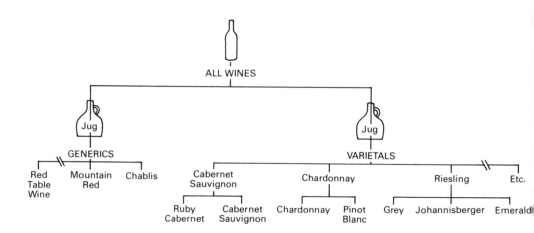

Let us leave this dry land of philosophy for more rewarding topics.

When you go out to buy a Médoc, a Château Haut-Batailley, for example, what you are really doing is deciding that you want a Cabernet Sauvignon. In California it's the reverse. You decide you want a Cabernet and then you choose the vineyard. And that is the way we should approach the field in California: Through the grape varieties.

First and most obvious are the blended wines. They are mixes of different grapes that produce a trustworthy beverage for heavy drinking. Gallo mixes prolifically-bearing clones of Petite Sirah, Carignane, Zinfandel and Barbera for its Hearty Burgundy. Inexpensive grapes make cheap wine. If you want more character you will have to pay more.

Names like Sauterns,* Mountain Red, etc., are vestiges of another era. They won't fade away, but their importance is decreasing. What is replacing them is jug varietals: Half gallons of straight Zinfandel and the like. This direct labeling is preferable. Terms like Mountain Red have no meaning, except perhaps to imply robustness. The grapes are as likely to come from the valley floor as the mountainside. When Sabastiani put out his first "mountain" wine, Beaulieu, in jest, retaliated with a "Mole Hill" wine—the joke being that Sebastiani was making a mountain out of a mole hill.

Currently there is a pleasant upsurge of honest wines simply labeled "red table wine." This trend is being fed by the greatly increased vine plantings of the late 1960s, and by the increased sophistication of a previously innocent audience. That "straight" Zinfandel, incidentally, will most likely be mixed with other grapes, because the present law says that only fifty-one percent of the grape listed on the label need be in the bottle.

Above these wines of commerce you have a coterie of mid-premium wineries. The emphasis switches from the product to the producer. The best of these are familiar names:

Group A	*Group B*
Inglenook	Paul Masson
Sebastiani	Wente
Louis Martini	Christian Bros.
Beaulieu	Krug
Mirassou	Weibel
Beringer	

---

* Note that for California, it is Sauterns; for France it is Sauternes.

The wineries in Group A are a large step ahead of the others in quality and usually in price as well. Their wines can be excellent, especially their reds. Cabernets are definitely the lions of their lines, and can be impressive wines, even ignoring their low (for California) prices of around $5.00. Each winery makes a Zinfandel. At around $3.00 they are good drinking wines with a hint of character. And all of the wineries, it seems, produce one odd varietal specialty wine that should be sought out. In Inglenook's case, it is the Charbono, a big, heavy fruity wine. Because it is undiscovered, it moves slowly on store shelves. That is both good and bad; older vintages which can still be a treat can be found, but on hot shelves they might also have spoiled. Risk it. Sebastiani's specialty is his Barbera. This is another powerful and pleasing fruit-filled red of northern-Italian origin. Louis Martini was always a pioneer in Merlot. He bottles some and uses the rest to soften his Cabernet, just as is done in Bordeaux.

If there is a common theme to wines from these wineries, it is that they are too smooth. They have a continuity of style that is almost predictable.* These wineries usually mix purchased and home-grown grapes, and this blending cancels out each area's unique character. Some not only mix grapes, but later blend different batches so as to give the public a wine that is consistent from year to year. There is much to say in favor of the practice. After all, all of France's great Champagnes are made this way and no one objects, but it does nothing for individuality. Individuality and excellence are still the center of our quest.

How loudly should we complain? Not very. These wines actually deserve our compliments. You can count on them. They will always be something you enjoy. They are well made by talented people who care. They have some complexity and, most important, theirs is a price you can afford. These are the bastions of dependability.

The top wines come from the boutique wineries which by way of unconventional definition is any West-Coast vineyard possessing only a single bathroom. This is of course unfair, but it does underline the fact that they are small.** All their energy goes into making wine. They seldom make more than three or four varieties. Almost all try their

---

* Especially Krug.

** Actually, enormous amounts of money go into even the most modest facilities and a few, such as Robert Mondavi, can ship a thousand cases a day. Even a small winery, one with a 25,000 gallon capacity, costs a minimum of $1,000,000 excluding land.

hand at Cabernet Sauvignon and Chardonnay, and most augment this small aristocracy with one other that can aspire to great heights, too: a Zinfandel, Petite Sirah or Chenin Blanc.

These wines distinguish themselves from others in California by occasionally establishing their own unique character. The results are as much an experiment as an art. As the winemaker shoots high, so too does he sometimes fall. I do not think that I have had a top-quality California wine that was actively bad as I have had from Europe. Instead, the worst tend to be disappointing for the price, which is usually high.

The existence of these small wineries is as much a product of rumor as it is of concrete presence in a wine store. Only a few, such as Simi, Ridge and Robert Mondavi, have achieved national distribution. These are the exception because normally quality is incompatible with size. To revise my previous definition to something more acceptable: A boutique winery is one which is small, ambitious and produces expensive wines.

As a thankless task I am including a list of some of the premium wineries you may have a chance to encounter:

Jos. Heitz	Robert Mondavi	Dry Creek
Mayacamas	Stags Leap	Fetzer
Simi	Schramsberg	Jos. Phelps
Souverain	Clos du Val	Spring Mountain
David Bruce	Callaway	Sterling
Ridge	Firestone	Grand Cru
Freemark Abbey	Chalone	Jos. Swann
Sutter Home	Ch. St. Jean	Ch. Montelena
Cuvaison	Mt. Veeder	Burgess
Chappellet	Hanzell	Mt. Eden

This begins to look like a telephone directory so I'll stop the list right here without prejudice to those not included.

In California, more than any other place in the world, a wine is a reflection of the man who made it. A vintner grows the grapes himself or chooses which ones he will buy. He vinifies the wine. He ages it. He bottles it. And his options at each juncture are enormous. Given identical grapes to begin with he can produce wines you couldn't identify as cousins. He could press one cluster immediately and let the other linger on the vine to increase its sugar content. After crushing,

	Cabernet Sauvignon	Pinot Noir	Zinfandel	Petite Sirah	Merlot	Gamay	Barbera	Others	Chardonnay	Pinot Blanc	White, Johannisberg Riesling	Grey Riesling	Fumé, Sauvignon Blanc	Chenin Blanc	Gewürztraminer	Others	Champagne
Almaden	•	•	•	•		•	•	•	•		•	•	•	•	•	•	•
Beaulieu	•	•				•			•		•		•			•	•
Beringer	•	•	•			•		•	•		•	•	•	•			
David Bruce	•	•	•						•								
Buena Vista	•	•	•						•		•	•				•	
Callaway	•			•							•		•	•			
Chalone		•							•					•			
Chappellet	•				•				•		•			•			
Charles Krug	•	•				•						•			•	•	
Ch. Montelena			•						•		•						
Christian Bros.	•	•	•			•			•					•		•	
Clos Duval	•		•														
Concannon	•		•	•									•				
Cuvaison															•		
Domaine Chandon																	•
Dry Creek	•		•						•				•				
Fetzer	•		•						•								
Firestone	•	•							•		•						
Konstantin Frank	•								•		•				•		
Freemark Abbey	•	•		•					•		•						
Hanzell		•							•								
Jos. Heitz	•		•				•	•	•		•						
Hoffman	•	•	•					•	•					•		•	
Hanns Kornell																	•
Inglenook	•	•	•	•		•		•	•		•	•	•	•	•		•
Kenwood	•	•				•											
Korbel	•	•		•													•
Llords & Elwood	•	•							•		•						
Louis Martini	•	•	•		•	•			•						•	•	
Paul Masson	•	•	•			•			•	•	•			•		•	
Mayacamas	•																
Jos. Phelps	•	•							•		•				•		
Mirassou	•		•			•			•	•	•			•	•		•
Robert Mondavi	•	•	•	•		•			•		•		•				
Mt Veeder	•								•								
Parducci	•	•	•	•		•			•						•		
Pedroncelli	•	•	•			•			•		•				•		
Ridge	•		•	•													
Ch. St. Jean	•								•		•						
Ste Michelle											•						
Schramsberg																	•
Sebastiani	•	•	•				•		•		•						
Simi	•	•	•					•	•		•				•		
Sonoma	•	•	•	•					•		•	•					
Souverain	•	•	•						•					•		•	
Spring Mt.	•								•	•			•				
Stag's Leap	•					•							•				
Jos. Swann		•															
Sterling	•		•		•				•					•		•	
Stony Hill									•		•						
Sutter Home																	
Weibel	•	•							•							•	•
Wente		•	•	•					•	•	•			•	•		

the first may be taken off the skins without leaving any pigmentation, the other stays on the lees for at least three weeks and gets a deep purple color. One will have tannin, the other little. Fermentation can take place hot or cool and that choice will affect the bouquet. Afterwards it can be aged in French oak, American oak or redwood and the cooperage (barrels) may be either 50 gallons or 500. Finally, one may stay in wood two years and the other five. The result will be wines that are totally dissimilar even though you started with identical grapes.

The result is that everybody is experimenting, and you will have a vast array of wines to choose from. With this number of options it is apparent you can do almost anything with a good grape. As an example of the variety which can be experienced, Zinfandel alone can be made into a white wine, an *oeil de perdrix*, a rosé, a light red, a great and powerful red, a late harvest and even a "beaujolais" type by carbonic maceration.

Novelty, however, isn't excellence. The grapes with the greatest potential remain our classic Cabernets and Chardonnays. I would put as the potential new additions Zinfandel, Chenin Blanc and perhaps Fumé (Sauvignon) Blanc.

Cabernet Sauvignon

It is clear who the leader is in California wines. It is Cabernet, so acknowledge it as king, but don't trust it. Many use its name in vain and denature its real worth, but when it is good, it is noble.

In 1964 California had only 1,612 acres of Cabernet. Ten years later this had grown to 25,000 acres. This means that there are very few older Cabernet vines in California and we already know that the age of a vine is a major determinant of quality. The average Cabernet vine was probably planted only in 1969, and obviously many of them must be even younger. After planting, it takes another four years for the plant to bear serviceable fruit and probably six more years before the real complexity starts to flow through. That is a full decade. Each succeeding year, the vines improve as the roots dig deeper into the soil, and each new vintage has the raw potential for being better than the one before it. As for now, however, only the best wineries or the oldest have access to the mature plants. The other vintners must use the maximum of their ample talents to imbue the younger vines with extra power. It makes one wonder if perhaps the youth of the vines is not one of the causes of California Cabernets seeming lighter than French Clarets.

There is another factor. A good many of the new vines were planted by growers, not wineries. The interests can be contrary. Growers want high production. Wineries want high quality. A winery owner like Bob Mondavi will beg his growers to leave the fruit on the vines a few extra days to get the maximum ripeness, but he doesn't own the land and the risk is not all his.

There is no way of knowing the age of the vines unless some honest soul puts it on his label, as the Mirassous do. Mostly you have to guess from its effect on the end product. A Clos du Val 1974 Cabernet Sauvignon is light and, considering the reputation of its winemaker—who is the son of the registeur of Château Lafite—its lightness must be due to the young vines he works with.

How can you tell what is going to be a good Cabernet? No one can, not from the outside at least. All you can determine, besides the vineyard's reputation, is the style to which the wine aspires, and for this I've designed the following tasting. Price is a possible tipoff but certainly not any guarantee.

TASTING 25: California Cabernet

For the low end, purchase either a red jug wine such as Gallo Hearty Burgundy, Gallo Ruby Cabernet or any similar wine that intrigues you for under $3.50 a bottle. For a mid-range premium try Inglenook Cabernet Sauvignon. Look for their "single cask" selections. Alternatively buy the regular Beaulieu Cabernet, but not the Private Reserve. Save that as the representative of the premium wine. Its full title is Beaulieu Cabernet Sauvignon Private Reserve George de Latour. It is made from a single vineyard of mature vines located in the floor of the Napa Valley. Another premium choice would be the Cabernet from Robert Mondavi. Lastly, for the most aspiring selection, try one of the boutique wineries such as Stags Leap, Ridge, Mayacamas, Chappellet, Caymus, etc.

However, before you buy any of these wines, it is time for a very important digression: Vintage years. Let us dispose of the myth right at the top. NOT EVERY YEAR IS A VINTAGE YEAR IN CALIFORNIA! If you buy a 1971 or 1972 you will see. Chances are you would be getting only half to two-thirds the quality you would have if you bought a 1970 or 1973—and you would be paying the same price. Perhaps the lows are not as bad as they are in Europe, but at least

SIMI

SINCE 1876

ALEXANDER VALLEY

PINOT NOIR
1973

Alcohol 12 % by Vol.
Produced and Bottled by SIMI Winery, Healdsburg, California, U.S.A.

Souverain
of Alexander Valley

GAMAY BEAUJOLAIS
NORTH COAST

produced & bottled at the winery by Souverain, Geyserville, Ca. Alcohol 13% by volume

KNIGHTS VALLEY ESTATE

Beringer® SINCE 1876

Sonoma

johannisberg riesling

Produced and bottled by
Beringer Vineyards, St. Helena, Napa Valley, California
Alcohol 12½% by Volume

Beringer®
Traubengold
A MEDIUM DRY CALIFORNIA RIESLING

Produced and bottled by
Beringer Vineyards, St. Helena, Napa Valley, California
Alcohol 12½% by Volume

there you would be paying much less for a disappointing vintage. Good California Cabernet costs at least $5.00 and sometimes in excess of $10.00, so guard yourself at least with the generalizations of this vintage chart. Like all charts it is an unfortunate simplification. Since most Cabernet is grown in the Napa and Sonoma valleys, it is based on the weather that prevailed there.

Year	Comment	Bordeaux	Rating (10 = highest)
1968	Big wines; very ripe, full-bodied style; quality uniformly excellent. Excellent aging potential.	1961	9–10
1969	Warm year; some very good wines, others were a bit thin; quality variable depending on crop size and location in valley.		7–8
1970	Big wines; ripe, fruity full-bodied style, small crop; wines uniformly excellent. Excellent aging potential.	1966, 1970	10
1971	Tannic, coarse wines, some a bit thin; quality variable, better in warmer Napa locations, some good wines made in North Valley; aging may improve, but lack body for long bottle aging.	1971	6–7
1972	Light, thin, low-alcohol wines in general. Good wines made from hillside grapes or other early-ripening locations harvested before rains. Quality highly variable, generally fair. Few wines will improve with age.	1967	4–5
1973	Most were good wines, some were great wines. Quality variable depending on crop size; weather was excellent. At best they are full-bodied, very fruity, soft and elegant. Good to excellent aging potential. Watch out for the occasional thin, lighter wine that resulted from overcropping.	1966, 1970	8–9
1974	Most were great wines, some were good, depending again on crop size. Generally bigger than '73s, fuller body, riper character.	1959, 1961	10

Year	Comment	Bordeaux	Rating (10 = highest)
	Watch out for a few very big Cabernets bottled with a scant two years age in the winery. These may not develop well in the bottle. In all other cases, they age well when bottled.		
1975	Some good wines, many were average, some were poor; cool year, some rain; best wines from warmest locations; wines will be light, fruity and delicate; few will be long lasting	1972	5–6
1976	A bit too early to evaluate; very big high-alcohol wines, in general; many seem unbalanced at this stage; some excellent wines will be made for sure! Very small crop, very high sugars in general (many *too* high); many vineyards ripened by dehydration (high sugar, high tannic acid and high pH). After fermentation, acids have dropped dramatically; time will tell.	?	?

The chart is predominantly oriented toward Cabernets, but it can be applied to the other grapes if you allow for healthy variations.

So buy the wines that interest you from the best of the years listed above. Conforming vintage dates is not important since style is what interests us, and this should carry over from one year to the next.

Preferred:
Low end: Gallo Hearty Burgundy
             Gallo Ruby Cabernet

Mid-Range: Inglenook Cabernet Sauvignon
               Beaulieu Cabernet Sauvignon

Premium: Beaulieu Cabernet Sauvignon Private Reserve
             Robert Mondavi Cabernet Sauvignon

Boutique: Stags Leap Cabernet Sauvignon
              Chappellet Cabernet Sauvignon
              Mayacamas Cabernet Sauvignon

Alternatives:
Low end: Any red jug wine or inexpensive (!) bottle

Mid-Range: Louis Martini Cabernet Sauvignon
Charles Krug Cabernet Sauvignon
Sebastiani Cabernet Sauvignon

Premium: Joseph Heitz Cabernet Sauvignon
Fetzer Cabernet Sauvignon
Simi Cabernet Sauvignon

Boutique: Ridge Cabernet Sauvignon
Freemark Abbey Cabernet Bosche
Caymus Cabernet Sauvignon

Optional: A 1970 or 1973 chateau-bottled grand cru wine from the
Médoc: Lynch-Bages, Ducru-Beaucaillou or that ilk.

Vintage: See vintage chart above.

Consumerism. I was disturbed by my 1968 Cabernets. They were said to be the greatest that California ever produced, but in less than a decade they were already at their peak and some were even beginning to fade. The wines were light and delicate, yes, but hardly with the power that California proclaims to be the equal of Bordeaux. What then was wrong? Nothing. It is just that California is changing so rapidly that the wines they produce today cannot be compared to even the best vintage of the 1960s. The wineries are vinifying them differently, trying for a deeper, longer-lasting wine. The trouble is that there are as yet no old wines. We have no history of what these new wines will become. We and they are guessing—and mixing in some wishful thinking as well. So don't take what writers say about Freemark Abbey outclassing an equally youthful Mouton-Rothschild as gospel. The truth is no one knows for sure what time will contribute to these wines.

Further comparisons to Bordeaux are inevitable. In the early 1970s modern brigandry was practiced in the Médoc when "futures" (pay now, receive later) for the poor 1969 crop went for $7.00 or $8.00 a bottle. At that time you could buy a lovely California Cabernet for $6.00, and so these small wineries filled a very necessary gap for us all. Now the situation has reversed itself. A respectable château-bottled wine can be found for $6.00, but the West-Coast wines are $8.00, $9.00 and $10.00. That seems high, yet there exists a market which happily supports them. We can complain about the value, but in the end we must pay if we want to enjoy them.

ZINFANDEL

It is possible that at the present time Zinfandel may be producing more fine wine in California than does Cabernet. There are more old vines. A good number of vineyards are twenty years old, and a few up to half a century. This will lend suppleness and breed to any premium grape. There are individual Cabernets of great promise, but a whole field of Zinfandel.

Much of Zinfandel's success can be attributed to its forgiving nature. It yields good color in almost any region. It seems intrinsically well balanced. It has such fruit, power, character and aging potential that one can fashion a unique wine from it.

When it is light and cheap, it is great for summer guzzling. It will always be a fruity mouthful. As the wine is made heavier, it grows in distinction until it takes on a character similar to a Claret. Some are actually fermented to seventeen and one-half percent alcohol naturally, and can only be compared to a port. In all, it is not a boring wine.

It differs from a Cabernet in that it is more earthy and less austere. That earthiness can make the wine rough, but even at equivalent levels of tannin it comes off as less astringent. It is also less dry and more fruity than a Cabernet, and makes one think of some of the big northern-Italian wines. The wine is usually palatable from the first. Aging improves the bouquet. The best Zinfandel is getting expensive; not as much as a Cabernet, but close.

Zinfandels ripen less precariously than do the Cabernets, so the vintage-chart comments can be taken less religiously. A number of good Zinfandels were made in 1972 by Clos du Val, Fetzer and Mayacamas, among others, though you will find better ones among the 1973s and the best in the 1974s.

If you are fortunate, the entire Zinfandel tasting can be done with one vineyard: Ridge. They have specialized in Zinfandel. They have over a half-dozen sites producing it, and they bottle each separately. Together they cover the whole spectrum of potential to realization. Each is worked to make the most of its attributes, and a comparison of even two of them is illuminating. Here you have one man using the same grapes but from two different soils. It's bound to be interesting.

As the alternative, buy the same full spectrum of quality as we did for the Cabernet tasting. If there is any jug wine left over from the "low end" bottle use it here. Its core will probably be Zinfandel any-way. There are also many half-gallon Zinfandels on the market, and these can be excellent daily wines. Next add a $2.00 to $3.50 bottle. Lastly, add one above $5.00. If your curiosity moves you, also include one of the "novelty" Zinfandels, such as a late harvest or a rosé.

TASTING 26: Zinfandel

Preferred:
Low-End: Los Hermanos Zinfandel

Mid-Range: Dry Creek Zinfandel

Premium: Ridge

Alternatives:
Low End: C. K. Mondavi

Mid-Range: Inglenook
Beaulieu
Krug

Premium: Joseph Swann
Clos du Val
Fetzer
Mayacamas

Optional: David Bruce Late Harvest Zinfandel
Grand Cru Vineyards Late Harvest Zinfandel
Concannon Zinfandel Rose
Any other novelty Zinfandel

CHARDONNAY

Occasionally one can point to a specific man and minute when a great wine was "invented." The late James Zellerbach, a multi-millionaire industrialist, opened Hanzel Winery in 1957. His chais* was a replica of the Clos Vougeot, and he wanted his wines to match. By harvesting his Chardonnay grapes later than was the custom, by fermenting the wines in artificially-cooled tanks for more accurate con-trol and by using small European oak barrels, he created a wine that was of Côte de Beaune quality. His pioneering lessons taught others, and today California Chardonnays are at least the equal of, and some

---

* The shed where the wine is stored while still in cask (French).

think superior to, any in the world. What is even more exciting is that this industry is just two decades old, and it is doubtful that all the best sites have been found. Europe is old and ossified in its traditions. Its vineyards cannot expand. California's can, and still hold quality. It is as if the world has suddenly been able to double or triple its supply of fine wine.

Chardonnay is too expensive a grape to use in bulk wines. If mass cultivated it loses its character, so you will only find it in premium wines. The least expensive will have up to forty-nine percent of other varieties added to stretch it. It is necessary to spend $4.00 or more before your purchase takes on equivalent value.

Chardonnays break down into two styles: One as big and robust as a twelve by twenty-four foot canvas by Rubens—something so grand it is almost bigger than life; the other is exquisite, a delicate, refined and elegant portrait by David.

The big ones have more alcohol, acid and are usually more strongly flavored with oak. They have a heavier body. The others are of lighter body with a clean tartness and layers of fresh, intense tastes.

See Tasting 22, page 147.

Consumerism. A word of warning: The elegant Chardonnays go well with all the traditional white meat and fish dishes, but the powerful Chardonnays sneer at food. They can be so big and complex that you should enjoy them unaccompanied, possibly after the meal but before dessert.

As to buying Chardonnays, there are few tricks. They are expensive and you must pay for them. If you have already done the French Chardonnay tasting complete with the optional American wines, then you know that above five and a half dollars they are at least as interesting and complex. Above nine dollars I have come to favor some of the Californias over even the greatest of the French, not the least because our wines stop at twelve or thirteen dollars and theirs go through the roof. If the five-dollar minimum seems a bit much, switch to any of the alternatives discussed below. You won't be disappointed.

Lastly, all premium California Chardonnays aspire to greatness. Let them age. Just because they are bottled and released early is no reason to believe that they are optimum. For a vintage like 1973 or 1974, six years does not seem unreasonable. The heavy and more powerful wines may take longer, but this is a new style and we have no experience with it.

CHENIN BLANC AND FRIENDS

Zinfandel follows in the shadows of Cabernet; Chenin Blanc in the shadow of Chardonnay. They are not the same but they have similarities. It is a left-handed compliment, but one can think of Chenin Blancs as a poor-man's Chardonnay. *Dry* Chenin Blancs are lovely, crisp and appealing. They carry some of the same breed and charm as the Chardonnay, but at a price that is frequently forty percent less. It would be particularly interesting to contrast Chappellet's Chardonnay to his lovely Chenin Blanc, to see how one man works with two similar grapes.

Another grape that has the potential for making great wine is the Fumé Blanc. It is also called the Sauvignon Blanc. Robert Mondavi was one of the earliest sponsors of this grape, and his Fumé Blanc is still the benchmark. The grape is the same as is used in white Bordeaux, Pouilly-Fumé and Sancerre. The original cuttings may even have come from Château d'Yquem, but in California the preferred style is dry. It is a racy wine with some of the austere elegance that characterizes a Chardonnay. At three to four and a half dollars a bottle you seem to be receiving a lot of quality for the money.

In both cases, for Chenin Blanc and for Fumé Blanc, be sure to purchase the dry styles. Sweet versions are also made, but cannot be compared with a dry Chardonnay. Read the label; it will tell.

Last, there is another grape being raised on the West Coast that is exceptional. It isn't compatible with these wines; in fact it stands apart from just about everything. It is the Gewürztraminer. It is a deeply-flowered and spicy wine. My first experience with it in Luxembourg convinced me it was made from fermented grapefruits—hardly a recommendation. But time has mellowed me and brought me better bottles. It reminds one of a Riesling but with more body and with that crisp spice that cuts through pungent foods. The versions from Simi and the Mirassous are exceptional wines. Tom Farrel of Inglenook thinks his 1973 is the best wine he has ever made. The future may show this to be a widely recommended varietal.

VIII

VALUE AND
DIVERSIONS

This is the last chapter and my last chance to have a spring cleaning. I have said as much as can profitably be said about each area for an introductory wine course, yet there are still things hanging about. Most of them relate to value, which in retrospect and to my surprise has turned out to be the leitmotif of this book. It surfaced because while writing I realized that you save money in wine (or any other field) by knowing something about it. If you don't learn about wines, then you will either buy the wrong wines—in which case your money is wasted—or you'll pay a lot extra for the security of knowing that what you've bought is good. That applies to all wines from Blue Nun to Château Lafite: You pay extra. Anyone who has tasted or even read this far is in a position to exercise personal judgment with confidence. What I would like to add are some observations about certain wines that are under-appreciated, and suggest some tasting games you might enjoy playing.

As I was in the middle of my first draft of this final chapter, Robert Daly came out with a superb article in the Sunday *New York Times*. His theme was that for every great château in the Médoc, there existed a neighbor less famous but of equal stature: That Haut-Brion meets its peer in La Mission-Haut-Brion; that Latour can be matched with

Léoville-Las-Cases; that Margaux has its rival in Palmer*; that Cheval Blanc is rivaled by Figeac, Ausone is on a level with La Gaffelière; and Pétrus can be challenged by La Conseillante. The famous wines cost two or three hundred percent more than their less well-known rivals. If everyone knew that these wines were roughly equal, who would pay the extra money? The point is that we all pay for what we do not know.

The reason that the wines are so similar is that each of the pairs of châteaux are contiguous. They share the same basic grapes, the weather is identical, and the key factor—the soil—is identical too. This means that the soil has to be something very special or else all surrounding wines would be the same. We must be working on two levels now. For example, there is an over-all sand and gravel composition that gives a certain style to all St. Émilions. And there is a unique limestone substrata which distinguishes only Ausone and La Gaffelière. The natural factors are not the only controls on quality. The two vineyards might have identical capacity for making perfect wine, but the one whose wine presently sells for more has the advantage of being able to afford to give more extensive care to his vines. This creates an artificial advantage because the distinction is caused by economics, not nature. If you want to buy a premier cru then you must pay the price, but with scarcely any difference in quality you can save a substantial amount by choosing the doppelgänger instead.

While we are rounding up facts about these first growths, it is interesting to note that most first growths have a "second" label. Château Latour also puts out Les Forts de Latour, which has no official classification. Some of the wine in the bottle comes from grapes that weren't up to the standards for a first-growth Latour bottling. The rest comes from new vines on the same estate, ones which haven't matured sufficiently to give them the desired depth, and vines from an additional parcel of reclaimed land that is part of the estate but not part of the classification of 1855.

Until 1967 Château Lafite had a similar label, Carruades de Lafite. It too supposedly contained wine from younger vines. Some of these are still available and they are an interesting "discount" way to indulge in a great name.

Château Palmer has as its second name Château Desmirail, whose land is now part of the Palmer property. Château Pichon Lalande has

---

* Here I think he stretched the point. It's not that Palmer isn't great but they rely on merlot while Latour uses cabernet so it's not equivalent.

Reserve de la Comtesse to absorb overproduction from its vineyards. Château Gloria has Haut-Beychevelle and Peymartin based on evaluation of individual barrels.

Some of the families who own great growths also own other châteaux. Lafite and Mouton protect their flanks by owning all the surrounding châteaux. The Mouton branch of the Rothschilds owns Château Mouton-Baron-Philippe and Château Clerc-Milon-Rothschild. Lafite has Château Duhart-Milon-Rothschild. Both try to capitalize on the prestige of the parent. Both have also significantly upgraded the quality of the old estates. Whether the name of Rothschild is worth the extra money they try to command is disputable. A case in point is Mouton Cadet, which incidentally isn't even a château. It is a commercially blended wine made from grapes grown anywhere in Bordeaux. To buy it and think you are getting a Rothschild is like buying a print instead of the original. A cru bourgeois would be more interesting.

The second-label syndrome is beginning to affect California as well. Gallo, of course, has more names than Gulf & Western. Serious wine companies indulge in the habit as well. It is a way to fill out their lines. Krug has C.K. and C.K. Mondavi. Inglenook has Navalle. Beaulieu has Beau Tour. Château Montelena has Silverado. Chapellet has Pritchard Hill. Stag's Leap has Hawks Nest. The entire list would be long and fast changing, as is everything in California. The second lines, especially in California, are trading down in quality in an attempt to capitalize on the firms' expertise and distribution channels and to broaden their markets. It is too early to judge the value to us of this emerging trend.

FAMOUS UNKNOWN AREAS

There is something sweeter about wines you discover yourself. It is a personal achievement and a compliment to you. One of the nicest ways to locate them is to look for what fashion has passed by. There are great wine areas that are ignored today. Probably the finest of them is Tokay in Hungary. This was the wine of the Hapsburgs and it has been in mourning since their departure from the historical scene. An "individual" wine is not suitable for mass manufacture, and postrevolution vintages of Tokay have not rivaled earlier examples. Nonetheless, today's Tokay is clearly in the class of a good Sauternes or perhaps even a fine one, and at a price that is very fair.

To compare a Tokay to a Sauternes or to an *auslese* or *beerenauslese* implies that it is a sweet dessert wine. As happens in France and Germany, Hungary's Furmin grape is attacked by the noble rot, and the wine has the luscious concentration that is typical of such wines. The wines come in three grades, corresponding to their relative sweetness. The large barrel in which they are aged has a capacity equal to five smaller tubs, or "puttonyos." A bottle labeled three putts (short for puttonyos) would contain sixty percent noble rot grapes; four putts, eighty percent; and five putts, one hundred percent, or the equivalent of a *beerenauslese*. The price for a five-putt Tokay Aszu is—incredibly —under $6.00.

There is one other level that is rarely seen. If there is a legend in wine in Hungary, it is the "eszencia." The stories told about it sound like fairy tales for children, and it is so scarce that it adds new meaning to the word rare. The finest of the botrytised* grapes are segregated and put into small oak casks from the bottom of which a single goose quill protrudes. The pressure of gravity alone presses down on them. There are no crushing feet, no hydraulic plates. Only that juice which flows freely from the grape and drips off the quill is used to make "eszencia." The juice may be sixty percent sugar. Now I ask you, what child would believe a romantic tale like that? Yet, basically, it is true. The juice most likely collects in the tubs as the grapes are brought in from the fields, but the natural weight is identical. Eszencia probably lives longer than any unfortified wine in the world. Bottles from 1811 are still alive and vital today. Except for a little that was released in 1964, the wine is unavailable. What is still made is used to add character to the Tokay Aszu.

Hungary's neighbor and old empire partner, Austria, also can be the home of under-appreciated wines. Most of the ones you will see from there are simple fresh and flowery white wines, the types drunk in the gardens of Grinzing outside Vienna. They share a common taste with light German Rieslings. A few, a very few, are made from late-harvest grapes, and those can be quite a bargain. I have seen an Austrian *trockenbeerenauslese* on sale here for under $7.00. Inflation has been at work here, too—it may be up to $8.00. A lot of work goes into that bottle for such a slim financial reward.

Not all bargains are to be found in Central Europe. We have already covered the little known values of fine Italian and Spanish Rioja

---

* Same as "edelfäule" or "noble rot" see p. 89.

wines. But there is one other section of Spain that we haven't mentioned.

Sometimes an area's potential finds its expression in one man who comes and works a small miracle on a region. Such a man was Baron Ricasoli who virtually invented Chianti thereby transforming what was formerly a pedestrian wine into a thing of beauty. A contemporary Baron Ricasoli may be a Californian named Jean Leon. Jean Leon decided that an obscure district of Spain, called Panades, had the potential to make great wines. He tore up the old vines and replaced them with cuttings from Château Margaux and Château Lafite. He rebuilt his cellars and replaced the vats and hand presses with temperature-controlled fermentation tanks. He also broke with more frugal Spanish traditions by aging his wine in expensive Limousin oak the same way it is done in Bordeaux. The result is one of the finest new wines I've had in years. In harmony and balance it can be mistaken for the best Beaulieu Private Reserve. One can hardly talk about a region based on one producer, but unless this is an isolated example, great varietal wines may be coming from Panades in the future.*

The Dao area of Portugal should also be added to the fine pre-inflation red wines. Its exports are small, but, like mushrooms, they occasionally pop up: A simple fifteen-year-old vino tinto for $3.00 here; a 1949 Pinot Noir for $6.00 there. Usually they appeal to people who prefer powerful dry wines. It is said that cigarette smokers like Riojas and cigar lovers prefer the Dao.

France is too much devoted to wines to be barren of bargains. Some of the well-known areas still have not been caught in the upward price spiral. Rhône Valley wines at prices of $3.00 to $7.00 are capable of being more complex and pleasant than their competition in Burgundy. Wines bearing town names are preferred to a simple Côtes-du-Rhône appellation. Hermitage is the most respected; Châteauneuf-du-Pape, the most well known; and Gigondas perhaps the best buy. The wines of Gigondas have a healthy reputation for integrity. These powerful, earthy red wines seem like a cross between the fine wines of northern Italy and those of the Côte d'Or. They are hard in youth with a heady bouquet that opens up in time to some elegance. The color is a much deeper purple than most Burgundies, and the taste is robust and lush.

The north of the Rhône valley is called the Côte Rôtie. Although obscure, some of its wines may be the best in the whole valley. They are

---

* Called "Jean Leon, Cabernet Sauvignon." Imported by Kobrand Corp.

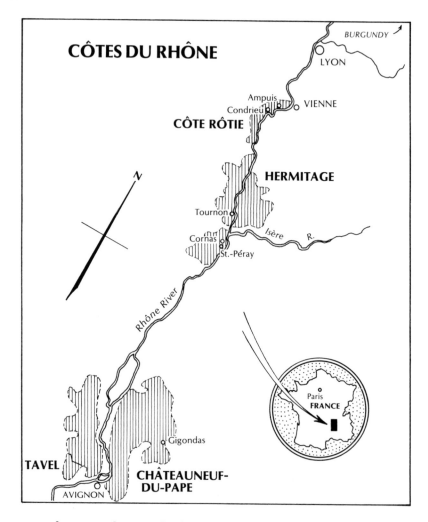

not as heavy as the ones further south, and thus are more elegant and have more finesse.

America, too, has its hidden secrets. One of the oddities of American winemaking is Dr. Konstantin Frank, a tenacious and gifted immigrant who insists that the greatest European-type wines can be grown in the Finger Lakes region of upper New York State. If you are just curious or have the mind of a collector, you should make a point of seeking out his wines. The man has great art. He has succeeded in making a *trockenbeerenauslese*. In fact, all his Rieslings are interesting, and so are his Chardonnays. In deference to a courageous old man we will not comment on his Cabernet.

Another man working in the alleys and byways is Walter Taylor. His family formerly owned Taylor Wine—now a subsidiary of Coca-Cola. He is now on his own. His attempt to shake the foundations of the United States wine industry consists in growing hybrid grapes. These are crosses of various European (*vinifera*) grape stocks with domestic (*labrusca*) vines to accent desirable characteristics and survive the crippling northeastern winters. Your reaction to his wines will be in proportion to your open-mindedness.

California is hardly a neglected area, but there are still bargains flowing from there. They cannot be easily categorized, because they are transient. You must learn the current ones from your local wine merchant. Right now my house wine is the Los Hermanos (that's Beringer) Chardonnay, a jug wine with good varietal character at a reasonable price.

Some of the better known California wineries also make a small quantity of West Coast "Champagne." Korbel is the most popular, and Almaden is surprisingly acceptable, but I prefer Beaulieu and Inglenook at the same or lower price. I have found that the vintage year is actually very important, so if you find one you like, follow the year as well as the brand. America has its premium sparkling wines as well: Mirassou natural, Schramsberg and Domaine Chandon. Each has its adherents. The Domaine Chandon in particular suffers from too much public relations hooey. It was made, as one of its executives admitted to me, for an absence of faults rather than for a positiveness of character. For $9.00 I'd rather buy a true Moët & Chandon.

In buying domestic sparkling wines, it is necessary to check the label. We use three methods to make "Champagne," and this defines its quality. The best uses the time-consuming techniques employed in making fine French Champagne, and its label will say "Fermented in *this* bottle." A slight drop in quality uses the bulk or charmat process and will say "fermented in *the* bottle." The last way is direct carbonation, and that isn't any good at all.

GAMES

Games are taste games. It is what happens when two people of similar interests sit down and try to amuse one another. It is a cross between an intellectual and a sensual puzzle where you try to unravel the riddles of the relationships in wine. It may start with the premise, "what happens when. . . ." What happens when they make a white wine from the pinot noir grape? So you go out and buy a white Nuits-St.-Georges and slip it undetected into a tasting.

Every tasting should have one ringer, say two bottles of the same wine or more curious, even three or four to show how much variation there can be even within the same case. This is especially true if the wine has been stored for a considerable length of time or shipped under dubious circumstances. A variant on this theme is showing the same wine purchased in Europe and another bottle from over here. When this was done to a group of us, we found that the European wine (which was flown over) was younger and more forceful. The American import was readier and more mellow. Perhaps the method of shipment (plane versus freighter) accounted for the difference.

Another useful diversion would be to compare neighboring chateaux. Two that I would suggest would be Château Léoville-Barton versus Château Langoa-Barton; and Château Latour against Pichon-Lalande, Pichon-Baron and Les Forts de Latour. There are different lessons to be learned.

Both of the Bartons are owned by the same man, Ronald Barton of the famous wine firm of B&G. The estates are contiguous; the grape mixes are roughly identical; the vines are of approximately the same age. Even the vigneron is the same. Nonetheless, as Cyril Ray the English wine commentator points out, the Langoa will mature a little more rapidly, remain at its peak for a shorter duration, and seldom achieve the delicacy or status of the Léoville. Some subtle change in the subsoil seems the only explanation.

If the grape blend had not been identical, then that would have been the logical place to start. That is why the second tasting was suggested. Again, all the chateaux are contiguous but are miles apart in taste. The key, naturally, is in the differing percentages of Cabernet and secondary grapes employed. Latour uses 75 percent Cabernet, which is why it is known for being an inky, tough, almost octagenarian wine. The Baron uses roughly 60 percent and the Lalande, a soft, lovely wine, uses 42 percent. These percentages are not a fixed chemical formula. They will be varied according to the dictates of the harvest. The Les Forts de Latour is included because it is made from the same grapes that make Château Latour, only it comes from younger vines or barrels not felt to be totally up to the Latour name. It may also come from parcels of the estate not covered in the 1855 classification—or at least that is what they tell us.

The following table can prove useful as a loose guide to the blending standards of some of the better known Bordeaux châteaux:

	% Cabernet Sauvignon	% Cabernet Franc	% Merlot	% Petit Verdot
Ausone	16	17	66	
Batailley	75		25	
Beauséjour	15	15	70	
Beau-Site	50	25	25	
Beychevelle	68	4	28	
Boyd-Cantenac	69	7	19	5
Brane-Cantenac	60	17	20	3
Calon-Ségur	33	33	33	
Canon	7	35	58	
Cantenac-Brown	50	20	30	
Chasse-Spleen	50	5	35	10
Cheval Blanc	30	30	40	
Close Fourtet	30	15	55	
Corbin	34	33	33	
Cos-d'Estournel	60		40	
De Pez	70	15	10	
Ducru-Beaucaillou	65	10	25	
Figeac	30	30	40	
Gazin	20	20	60	
Giscours	50	25	20	5
Grand-Puy-Lacoste	75		25	
Gruaud-Larose	70	5	20	5
Haut-Bailly	50		50	
Haut-Brion	55	25	20	
La Conseillante		55	45	
Lafite-Rothschild	63	15	18	4
Lafon-Rochet	60		40	
La Mission-Haut-Brion	60	10	30	
Langoa-Barton	75		20	5
Lanessan	60		40	
Lascombes	45	11	32	10
Latour	75	15	8	2
Léoville-Barton	75		20	5
Léoville-Las-Cases	70	15	15	
Léoville-Poyferré	50		50	
L'Évangile		33	67	
Loudenne	47	8	45	

	% Cabernet Sauvignon	% Cabernet Franc	% Merlot	% Petit Verdot
Lynch-Bages	60	25	15	
Margaux	75		25	
Montrose	65	10	15	
Mouton-Rothschild	90	7	3	
Palmer	75		25	
Pavie	15	25	60	
Petit-Village	10	15	70	5
Pétrus	7		93	
Pichon-Lalande	42	14	36	8
Pichon-Baron-Longueville	60	5	30	5
Pontet-Canet	75	2	23	
Prieuré-Lichine	50	5	40	5
Rausan-Ségla	50	10	35	5
Smith-Haut-Lafitte	70	5	25	
Talbot	70	3	25	2
Trottevieille		75	25	
Vieux-Château-Certan	20	30	50	

You can invent hundreds of similar games for California wines. You may want to see the amazing things that can be done with Zinfandels. As we know, it makes everything from a white wine to a seventeen and one-half percent-alcohol red. Or you may want to contrast Robert Mondavi's unfiltered Cabernet with his filtered, to see if as much character is lost in the filtration as some people claim. And so on.

There is another game, and that is the game that tends to be played on you. It is the snobbery game: The intimidating waiter; the cold maître d'; the overpriced wine list; and finally the bad bottle. How you handle it is a matter of your own temperament. My father, who can get away with anything, once sent a bottle back because it was "bottled too near the cork"—a meaningless remark properly used to chastise a pretentious waiter. Incidentally, the wine was bad—but not for that reason. Another technique to unbalance a waiter who doesn't know Champagne from ginger ale is to look deeply into the glass, frown and say "bunions!"—a remark intimating that the foot that trod the grapes was flawed. After the second bottle foolish remarks come more easily.

When the wine is legitimately spoiled, send it back. If you have read this far you know more than all but an appallingly few restaurateurs.

In fact, if there is anything that should give you confidence in your own growing knowledge, it is the mediocrity of almost every wine list.

There is no cure for a bad or over-priced wine list except Perrier or non-patronage. Perrier is a face-saving choice. It has the cachet of Champagne and the price of a watery drink. If you feel that a meal without wine is as unattractive a prospect as dieting, then opt for the third least expensive wine on the list. The bottom two are specifically chosen for their long mark-up and thus are poor value. Also, unless the restaurant is known for its wine selection or someone is obviously knowledgeable, don't ask the waiter. It is depressing how little he knows. As we have seen, it is not hard to find bargains, so why don't *they* do it?

SHERRY

The image of sherry, spurred by the bulk California counterfeiters, is that of a viscous sweet wine—a gentile Mogen David. The truth is delightfully different. It is wine of the highest quality. The fine sherries of Spain will range from bone dry, fresh and nutty to more full-bodied, richer wines—but will *never* approximate that cloying commercial stuff used in cooking. With the light and dry revolution hard upon us, let us hope that fine sherry will become more popular and available.

Sherry has an appeal that is unique. Its appeal stems from two factors: The way it is made and the way it is aged. The grape is a new one for us, the Palomino. It is made into wine in the usual manner, but whereas most wines turn to vinegar when they come into contact with the air, Sherry develops a protective "skin." The skin comes from *flor*, a mysterious, beneficial yeast strain borne on the winds. The comings and goings of the *flor* are uncontrollable and ill understood. In the barrels it grows to cover the top of the wine with a white, unattractive scum, fairly thick and hard to pierce. For as long as it is present, the wine will not oxidize but will gain the benefit of age and take on a nutty, yeast-like flavor. The wine does not stay on the *flor* forever, but it later *solera*-aged and blended.

There are three major types of sherry: *Fino Amontillado* and *Oloroso*. It is up to the wine to decide which it wants to be. Once the wine is fermented, if the *flor* forms and if the resulting wine has great potential, it is marked to become *Fino*. *Fino* is the best. It is appetizing, fresh, delicate and rather nutty, with great finesse, but almost austerely dry.

A *Fino* that is allowed to age in the cask and not treated to the *solera* method of fractional blending will become an *Amontillado*. It is stronger in alcohol but more mellow to the taste than *Fino*, and because of the different treatment in wood, there will be a more perceptible feeling of age.

Imagine a cascade; a series of pools arranged such that as the topmost is filled, its overflow is caught in the one below, and when that one fills, it flows into the one below it, and so on. Thus all are kept topped up by the perpetual addition to the topmost or youngest pool. That is fundamentally how the *solera* system works. Usually a series of casks are established one over the other. As wine is drawn off for bottling

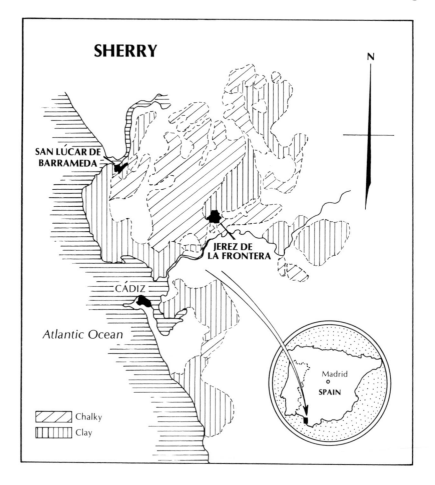

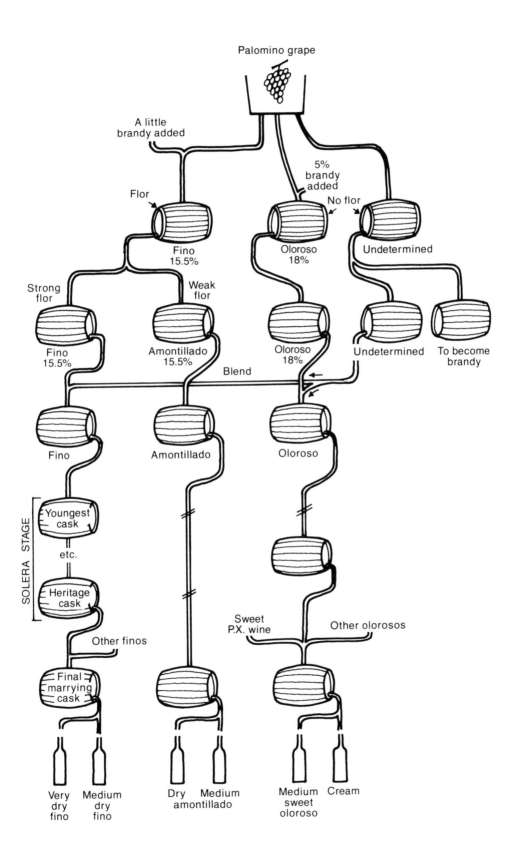

from the oldest and bottom-most, it is replaced with an equal amount from the cask above it. The casks are not filled to the top, so there is room for the *flor*. The top cask is replenished with new wine. The result is that the bottom cask will always contain the oldest wine of a uniform quality that is refreshed each time with younger, more vital wine from above. This process gives a wonderful combination of age, freshness and consistency. *Soleras* like this can be established for a hundred years or more, but this is no guarantee that the wine drawn out of the bottom is that old; only a small percentage is, but the system works to give it much of the character of old wood and great age.

There is one final step. Each of the soleras has its own style. Some may be older, some more delicate, some rough and fresh, etc. As in Champagne, the choice is to blend for the best balance of characteristics. So when the wine is pulled from the heritage cask, it is mixed with others and allowed to marry in a new cask before bottling. By varying the blend it is possible to create any quality level *Fino, Oloroso* or *Amontillado*, one to meet any market or purse.

Consumerism. It is not hard to predict that good *Finos* will become increasingly popular substitutes for cocktails. They are easy to drink, deceptively strong and not filling. The famous shippers like Harveys, Sandeman and Gonzalez Byass can always be relied upon. However, their prices can be undercut by experimenting with some of the less well known but still reputable names like Wisdom & Warter.

PORT

If the French like their wines too young and the English like theirs too old, then port clearly sides with the English. In unromantic terms, port is a wine made from any combination of traditional grapes whose fermentation has been retarded when only half complete by a large dose of brandy. The brandy stuns and asphyxiates the yeast, thereby leaving the wine still rich in natural sugar. The resulting wine, usually red but occasionally white too, is sweet and high in alcohol.

As in Champagne there is vintage and nonvintage port. One year in three is regarded as special enough to be held apart for two years in wood and then bottled. In the bottle it will age fifteen or more additional years to approach maturity. This is vintage port. Nonvintage port obviously bears no vintage date and is treated differently.

Nonvintage port, again like Champagne, is a blend of several years. There are two major types: Ruby and tawny. Ruby is young, fresh and rather fruity. It is pleasant, perhaps harsh but not special. The tawny, nonvintage, stays in the barrels for many years. Like all old red wines it slowly loses its color and turns pale, hence its name, tawny. It will be drier, more elegant and mellow than vintage port. Only vintage and a fine old tawny will be great wines.

Vintage port has a big disadvantage. Because of the way it is made, its very deep color, the heavy tannic quality and the interrupted fermentation, it throws a very heavy sediment. This crust adheres to the side of the bottle. If shaken, it floats into the wine and takes a long time to settle out. It is unpleasant, but there is no simple way around it. Now some shippers keep the vintage in barrels for eight years (remem-

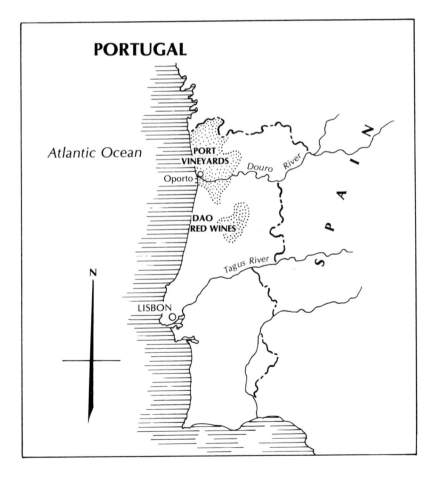

ber, usually it is only two) before bottling it. By that time it has thrown its deposit and can be bottled clear. The extra time in casks alters its absorption of wood flavors and oxygen. The result is a hybrid—good but not capable of aging like a true vintage port. It is labelled "late bottled."

MADEIRA

For a time, what port meant to the British, Madeira meant to the Americans. In its heyday, Madeira was the ultimate after-dinner drink: Old, rich and luscious. Its stature was eclipsed by two acts of nature. In the nineteenth century the vines were totally destroyed by successive waves of oidium (a disease) and then phylloxera (a parasite).* The struggle to rebuild lasted a generation but was generally accomplished by the turn of the century.

The fates of port and Madeira seem intertwined. Each owes its character to some special process. In port it is the heavy dose of brandy that stops fermentation. In Madeira it is the heat of the island and the long hot rolling sea voyage that was at one time required to deliver Madeira from the island to its final destination. The roll of the sailing ships and the heat of the hold mellowed and speeded the maturity of the wine. The constant shifting gave it more access to air.

The other quality that port and Madeira share is the addition of brandy. Only a small amount is added to Madeira and it would remain just brandy and wine if it were drunk quickly. But something happens: It happens in Champagne; it happens in sherry; and it happens in port as well. Over time because the brandy and the wine both come from grapes, the tastes meld and marry.

Nowadays there are no sailing ships to slowly warm, roll and age the wines, so the *bodegas* have to simulate the process. The casks of wine are put into large temperature-controlled tanks. The heat is gradually increased to around 110°F. and held there for three to six months, depending upon the quality desired. In the last month the temperature is slowly returned to normal. This is the *estufade* method. Some Madeira, however, is made without the heating, and the dif-

---

* Oidium was a fungal parasite similar to mildew which ruined the vineyards and devastated Europe and Madeira in the 1850s. The phylloxera did even worse damage 20 years later. It was an agricultural pest, imported by some foolish bug collector, which escaped and eventually almost wiped out European vine growing.

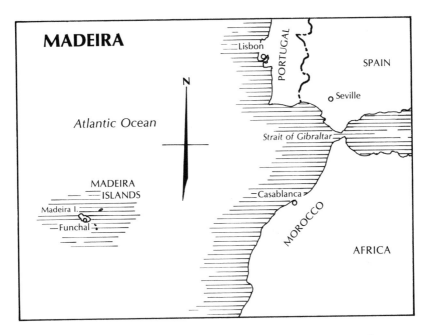

MADEIRA

Atlantic Ocean

MADEIRA ISLANDS

Madeira I.

Funchal

PORTUGAL

Lisbon

SPAIN

Seville

Strait of Gibraltar

Casablanca

MOROCCO

AFRICA

ference is quite remarkable. That wine is cherry red, harsh and aggressively fruity, with some raw alcohol smells that (while still eight months old) can snap your nose off. The more processed wine has gained a mahogany color and a more restrained, mellow taste.

Madeiras vary from dry to very rich depending upon the grape used. Starting with the driest, they go *Sercial, Verdelho, Bual* and *Malmsey*, which are also the names of the grapes.* Many people regard the first and the last as the best, but perhaps because of the facts cited in the footnote, it seems to me that the Verdelhos have been coming off better than the Sercials, and an old Bual is a wonderful wine too.

The Sercial can be compared to a fine, nutty Amontillado. Like the Sherry, it is a good appetizer alone or with soup. A Malmsey is too rich, sophisticated and well scented to go with a dinner. It is best afterward with a simple pound cake dessert.

Vintage dating is pretty straightforward on the island. The date shown on the bottle should be the date the wine was made. *Solera* wines are no longer allowed into the United States, though a few might remain on the shelves. *Solera* is now just marked "reserve," and bears

* In truth, a wine marked Sercial, Verdelho, etc., probably does not contain much of those grapes. Over the years the farmer probably let the vineyards containing those difficult-to-grow grapes deteriorate, and so wines blended to the same style were permitted to use that name. By law, when vineyards grow old now they must be replaced by these premium varieties. No substitutes will be accepted.

no date. There can be one cause of confusion. In 1972 the Portuguese government made the *bodegas* declare all the wines they kept in stock. If the *bodega* declared that a wine was 1904, it was accepted as official. The *bodega* owners are honest, but there could have been some minor imprecision. Still the difference of a year or five years in a wine that old is minimal.

COGNAC

To me it seems that there is fine Cognac and bad brandy with little in between. A concession must be made to include Armagnac which in its best moments can be better than cognac. Marc, Metaxa and Cardenal Mendoza have their followings as well, but really there is Cognac and then there is everything else.

All of these belong to the same family of distilled wines. Wine is made in the usual fashion from grapes. To call the basic wine itself undistinguished would be to exaggerate its good points. Something has to be done to improve it, so it is distilled. The wine starts out low in alcohol (7%) and high in acid, rather unpalatable. These initial proportions are actually an advantage. They permit the producers to concentrate the grape taste proportionately more than the increase in alcohol.* The trick of distillation is that water boils at a higher temperature than alcohol. So by raising the temperature of the wine, you can volatilize the alcohol and essential grape tastes but leave the water behind.

The distillation is a two-stage process. Each time the wine (now called *eau-de-vie*) goes through the still, it is divided into three batches. Only the middle one, the heart, is used. The head, which is the first part to boil away, is too sharp and pungent to be included, and the tail not enough. The heart is re-distilled and again only the central portion is used. The result is a colorless liquid that is too raw to drink. Ideally only time and oak are needed after this.

Cognac is not made by the large shipping firms but by thousands of local farmers. They grow the grapes. They make the wine. In most cases they distill the eau-de-vie. What they can't do is afford to age the Cognac, so they sell it to the large houses like Courvoisier or Remy Martin. These firms buy the raw Cognac from farmers located all over

---

* A 20% wine could only be concentrated five times to reach 100%. A 7% wine can be concentrated 14.2 times. Thus, the flavor concentration will be higher.

the delineated region. Each subregion has different taste characteristics, and these carry through to the eau-de-vie. As in Champagne and Chablis, the best soil is heavy with chalk and lime. The soil mix determines the desirability of the subregions. The best is the innermost, and that is Grande Champagne. Next is Petite Champagne. There are four others, but their names aren't important. The large firms buy from all the regions and store the casks in their warehouses. Most Cognac we buy is a blend not only of individual Cognacs from each of these regions, but also of Cognacs of different ages. The minimum age of the youngest eau-de-vie in a blend will never be less than three years, and there will be small batches with considerably more.

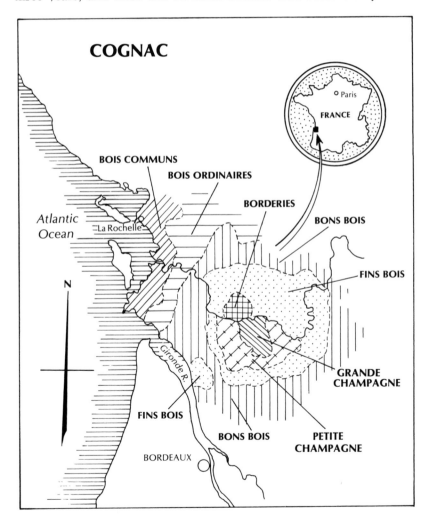

A vintage date on a Cognac is seldom meaningful, but occasionally you may see one if the unblended cask has been shipped to England and stored apart. More often you will see a label saying "Fine Champagne" or "Grande Fine Champagne," which means that the Cognac comes only from grapes grown in the two best districts. This is definitely superior and usually more costly than the wider blends.

You have to be a cryptographer to translate the symbols on most cognac bottles. What do they mean: V.S., V.S.O.P.,* Napoleon, one star, two stars, X.O., etc.? They mean very little, because they vary from house to house. The only rules you can go by are that "V.S." or "three star" must be at least three years old and that "V.S.O.P." at least five. Names like Napoleon do not imply vintage 1812. It just means an older blend. Fancy names like Paradise or Heritage are usually the oldest the shipper will part with, and they are as expensive as they are rare. The expense comes from two factors: The cost of money and the rate of evaporation. Because Cognac is so high in alcohol and because it is aged in Limousin oak—which is slowly permeable—the amount of evaporation is incredible. It is estimated that more than twenty-five thousand bottles a day are lost to "the angels' share."

To show why Cognac is so expensive I worked out the following table. I do not know if the assumptions are correct, but even if they are exaggerated, you will get a good idea of the dynamics involved. I assume that the original distilled cognac costs $2.00 per bottle, that money costs twelve percent compounded on an opportunity-cost basis and that six percent of the cognac is lost each year by evaporation.**

Year	a Cost	b Quantity Remaining	$(100 \div b)\ x_{a=d}$ Cost to Make One Bottle
0	$ 2.00	100%	$ 2.00
1	$ 2.24	94%	$ 2.38
5	$ 3.52	73%	$ 4.82
10	$ 6.21	53%	$11.71
15	$10.95	39%	$29.07
20	$19.29	29%	$66.51

---

* Somewhere Voltaire pointed out that the Holy Roman Empire wasn't very holy, wasn't Roman, and wasn't an Empire. Well, V.S.O.P. which stands for "very superior old pale" may be superior, but not very. It is not old and certainly is not pale. To mount curiosity on curiosity, note that the V.S.O.P. initials are for English not French words.

** Opportunity cost is a finance term meaning what the money would yield if employed in a different but typical investment.

In other words, it cost the producer over $66.00 for a true bottle of twenty-year-old-cognac. Profit and middleman charges would mean that you would pay more than $130.00. Ouch.

The trade keeps the price down by blending. Fortunately, a relatively small amount of aged Cognac will add character to a larger amount of younger Cognac. Another way is to hasten the effects of aging. When in cask, the wood mellows the harshness (the esters and aldehydes have a chance to mellow the fine bouquet) and wood also helps draw in moisture from the atmosphere, which lowers the alcohol level. Oak also adds color. Much of this can be accomplished in other ways. The air of the town of Cognac smells vaguely of caramel, because burnt sugar is added to young Cognac to darken it and give it the appearance of age. The slight sweetness mellows it. The practice is nearly ubiquitous and, while not desirable, it is practical. Another shortcut is to add distilled water thus replacing the more time-consuming air-dilution method. To some extent these shortcuts have hurt the quality of Cognac but the quality of the average bottle still remains fairly high.

One other point about Cognac that has been generally ignored is that the styles of the major shippers vary substantially. Some are light and elegant. Some are heavy and full. The light ones tend to appeal to people who like austere tastes. The heavier ones are softer and perhaps a bit more sweet.

Light	Medium	Heavy
Delamain	Bisquit	Courvoisier
Denis Mounie	Hennessy	Fontpinot
Hine		Martell
Remy Martin		
Ragnaud		

EPILOGUE

It is very difficult to end a book. It is hard to discipline oneself and say, "I have covered enough," but I have. The only thing I have left out are a few short observations.

Wine should not be treated as a museum object, held at a distance and prodded with intellectual fingers. You must be involved with it. Drink it. Interact. Above all, enjoy it. If we analyze things too much we lose the pleasure of the act and become technicians. A technician is one who can break a wine down into its component parts, its levels of tannin and volatile acidity, its grape, vintage, perhaps even its origin, but who has lost his or her ability to just plain react honestly to the wine. A professional may have to constantly analyze, but it is the advantage of us amateurs to know and enjoy the wine.

The partner of the technician is the collector. Strangest of all to me is the collector of wine, for he is like Midas who amasses without consuming. Wine gives great pleasure, and when we have an unusually fine bottle in our closet it makes no sense to pull it out for just any small occasion or for people who won't appreciate it. But there is a temptation to hoard that wine because there is more pleasure in a full bottle than an empty one. After a while that one bottle becomes a seed crystal and there is a whole bunch you won't touch. If they are ready, well damn it, get out there and drink them.

The nemesis of people who enjoy and know something about wine is the self-appointed deflator. He is the one who thrusts a glass of sherry drenched in lemon peel under your nose at a cocktail party and loudly demands that you identify it. Or he pours Manischewitz Honey Wine (which oddly enough is surprisingly good) into a Sauternes bottle with the intention of having you make an ass of yourself. These people are an unfortunate by-product of the snobberies and pretensions of wine, and in their own way are reacting against it. Their motivations are the key thing. Deceit is hostile and aggressive if the purpose is strictly to make the other person look foolish. But the same games can be very valuable to us all (keeping us humble renews our perspective), providing the intent is first to mystify and then to enlighten. Wine is fun, so keep light.

INDEX